THE WESTERN HORSE

THE WESTERN HORSE

A Popular History of the Wild and Working Animal

RANDI SAMUELSON-BROWN

TWODOT®

ESSEX, CONNECTICUT
HELENA, MONTANA

A · TWODOT® · BOOK

An imprint of Globe Pequot, the trade division of
The Globe Pequot Publishing Group, Inc.
64 South Main Street
Essex, CT 06426
www.globepequot.com

Distributed by NATIONAL BOOK NETWORK

British Library Cataloguing in Publication Information available

Library of Congress Cataloging-in-Publication Data
Names: Samuelson-Brown, Randi, author.
Title: The western horse : a popular history of the wild and working animal / Randi Samuelson-Brown.
Description: Essex, Connecticut : TwoDot, [2024] | Includes bibliographical references.
Identifiers: LCCN 2024008334 (print) | LCCN 2024008335 (ebook) | ISBN 9781493073849 (paperback) | ISBN 9781493073856 (ebook)
Subjects: LCSH: Horses—West (U.S.)—History. | Western horses—History.
Classification: LCC SF284.U5 S26 2024 (print) | LCC SF284.U5 (ebook) | DDC 636.100978—dc23/eng/20240517
LC record available at https://lccn.loc.gov/2024008334
LC ebook record available at https://lccn.loc.gov/2024008335

∞™ The paper used in this publication meets the minimum requirements of American National Standard for Information Sciences—Permanence of Paper for Printed Library Materials, ANSI/ NISO Z39.48-1992.

CONTENTS

Nothing stirs the soul as much as when a horse calls for you.

INTRODUCTION

Imagine a herd of wild Mustangs in Wyoming, manes dancing in the wind as storm clouds roll over the mountains. The wind rushes down the slopes, catching in the pines and hastening toward the valley floor. One of the Mustangs, a blood bay, lifts his head and calls. In the space of a few heartbeats, four or five horses begin running, slow at first then faster—manes and tails streaming out behind them like ribbons. Their necks and legs stretching and reaching. Hooves thudding. Soon, all the horses join in the race like a multicolored flowing stream—brown, grullo, black, and buckskin dashing across the distance. Running in the wind for the sheer joy coursing through their blood. Running to race the storm.

The legacy of the horse has been etched upon the western United States in many different ways. Place names—often remote—scattered throughout the western states tell the story: Spotted Horse (Wyoming), Wild Horse (Colorado), Hungry Horse (Montana), Bronco (California), Gray Horse (Oklahoma), Whitehorse (South Dakota), Horse Thief Canyon (in any variety of western states), Dead Horse Point (Utah), Mustang (Oklahoma and California), and the list goes on. Spur (Texas), Roundup (Montana), Corral City (Texas), and Corrales (New Mexico) all attest to the impact the western horse has made upon the land and the inhabitants of the West. The horse is a living historical legacy to be cherished and still valued today. Helpmeet, partner, savior, and occasional enemy, the horse remains an enduring icon of the West unlike any other. As Frank Thomas of Ford Motors Market Research explained, the trademark *Mustang* rose to the top "because it had the excitement of the wide-open spaces and was American as all hell."[1]

From the beginnings of time when the *Eohippus* or "dawn horse" emerged, to the herds that developed from escaped Spanish settlements, the horse is in many ways the lifeblood of the western region. Nowhere is the impact of the horse more readily seen upon an entire culture as that of the Plains tribes. Previously pedestrian, once the tribes became accustomed to the horse, learned how to ride, and harnessed the horses' strength, their lifestyles rapidly changed to that of a mounted culture reaching magnificent proportions. No matter the specific tribal affiliation, horse ownership conveyed status and wealth upon their owner and people. Raids were carried out for economic gain, to prove young men's bravery, and to control desired territory.

Of course, nothing in life is the same for everyone. In the Pueblo cultures, the horse was originally viewed as akin to a pest who ate their carefully cultivated crops. Although the Pueblo peoples never came to be considered as a truly mounted culture, they were shrewd enough to trade the horses to neighboring tribes and used them as a form of currency.

As time progressed, the US Cavalry would establish forts and outposts, patrolling those vast distances in those Indigenous tribe's territories as gold seekers and settlers hastened westward. If those seekers and settlers had not had access to the horse, the sheer distances of the sprawling landscape would have made significant settlement both exceedingly difficult and excruciatingly slow. It wouldn't be an overstatement to say that the horse was a driving force in the West, second only to man in his impact. Without the horse, tribes would have remained on foot, and the settlers would have primarily remained near their existing towns. Expansion would have been a much slower process, only allowing for a more gradual settlement as access to essential supplies allowed.

Between the Indigenous tribes and the encroaching settlers and miners (and therefore the US government), hostilities erupted. Again, the horse was pressed into service as an instrument of war on all sides. As horrific clashes were waged, horses were often collateral damage. Still, the settlement of the West progressed. There were the brief, shining moments of the Pony Express, a daring idea that covered over eighteen hundred miles to deliver news in ten days proving, once again, that anything was possible with good old American ingenuity.

A lone cowboy and his horse look over his horse herd (cavy).
PHOTO ERWIN E. SMITH (LIBRARY OF CONGRESS).

Ranchers, cowboys, saddle makers, stagecoach drivers, teamsters, freighters, and many others came into the West with a clear dependence upon the horse. Crime followed. Horse theft was a serious offense in its day, and still is. Historically referred to as the larceny of livestock, such thefts were at first dealt with by vigilantes. Even as law became established, resorting to "immediate" justice did not prove rare even in the later part of the nineteenth century. The loss or theft of a horse could lead to the death of either the victim or the criminal, and sometimes both.

Of course, their cause of demise differed.

Through all of this riding, settling, fighting, and struggling that comprised life out West, certain rides, horses, and riders became legendary. Other heroic rides and dramatic dashes have been swallowed up and forgotten over time. This account hopes to bring some of those heroic deeds (both human and equine) back to life, and to share some of the legends that arose from true events now faded from memory. Those western long-distance rides might not have held the staying power of Paul Revere's Midnight Ride, but they meant just as much (if not more) to the people dependent upon those fights-for-survival rides and danger-filled dashes over difficult terrain and circumstances.

Out of this heritage and history, the most American of sports, rodeo, originated. While this book cannot hope to cover all aspects of equines in the West, it seeks to place the spotlight on the horse who deserves prominence at the heart of the westward movement, and rightfully deserves a recognition in the history of the American West.

NOTE

1. Jake Lingeman, "Pony Magic: The History of the Mustang Logo,"*Autoweek*, April 27, 2020, https://www.autoweek.com/car-life/classic-cars/a32266716/history-of-the-mustang-logo.

CHAPTER 1

THE ORIGINS OF THE HORSE IN THE WESTERN UNITED STATES

THE EXISTENCE OF THE NORTH AMERICAN HORSE IS ONE OF THE greatest comeback stories of all times. The origins of wild horses on the North American continent go back at least fifty million years. Those early horses were not the large, awe-inspiring equines that we know today, but were diminutive in size and measured only about twelve inches tall. Those early horses are known as *Eohippus* or the "dawn horse," and they evolved into *Epihippus*, which evolved into other variants—all of which were native to the North American landmass. There are accounts that detail their evolution in much greater detail, but *Epihippus* eventually evolved into the *Pliohippus*, which is the direct predecessor of today's *Equus*. The *Equus*, or horse, evolved between one and four million years ago and stood about thirteen hands high at the withers, which translates into fifty-two inches. Five million years ago, the world had a different climate. The grasslands of the North American mid-continent had more rain than today, providing a lush environment hosting many varieties of vegetation and hoofed mammals. The *Equus* spread from coast to coast over time, undergoing physical changes and modifications as they evolved to match their environment. The earliest species had a narrow skull with a shorter snout. Soon, those snouts lengthened and became what is known as *Equus simplicidens*, commonly referred to as the Hagerman horse.

These grew to a slightly taller height of approximately fifteen hands at the withers. The remains of those early horses are predominantly found in the state of Idaho, at the site of a massive fossil bed deposit discovered in 1928. However, similar forms are found throughout the grassy parts of North America, including the state of Texas, albeit nothing matches in quantity to Idaho's fossil beds.

The next genus of note came in the form of a medium-sized California species called *Equus stenosis*.[1] Some of the *Equus stenosis* crossed over the Bering Land Bridge into Asia 1.8 million years ago. There they grazed upon the western Eurasian steppes where forage was plentiful and hunters few. The oldest fossils discovered in North America to this point in time, and which could belong to the *Equus caballus*, were discovered in volcanic ash beds in northeastern Nebraska in 1992. Now known as the Ashfall Fossil Beds near Royal, the remains of two stallions, a mare, and a foal have been unearthed. Dependent upon the skeleton, one- and three-toed horses were caught in an enormous eruption approximately twelve million years ago.[2]

This migration of the horses over the Bering Straits proved to be a fortunate event in hindsight. Horses became extinct in North America for unknown reasons eleven thousand years ago, toward the end of the last Ice Age. Researchers have expressed theories accounting for their extinction from the North American landmass ranging from the possibility that the *Equus* were hunted to extinction by early man or that they fell victim to climate change or disease. Any combination thereof might prove accurate as well. What is known is that from Asia, the horse spread into eastern Europe. In time, they became domesticated, used in warfare and agriculture, and were recognized as a valued commodity. Horses would not return to the New World until 1494 when they accompanied the Spanish explorers.

THE EXPLORERS

No horses accompanied Christopher Columbus when he set sail on his first voyage in 1492. Asia was Columbus' intended destination at the time, and he sailed in the hope of establishing a lucrative trade route for the Spanish crown and country. At that time, the location of Asia remained unknown, as did the distance. Whatever waited for the explorer and his men remained uncertain. As everyone knows, Columbus never made it to Asia for his riches. Instead, he found the "New World"—landing somewhere in the Bahamas and upon an island whose exact location has been lost to time. According to accounts from that voyage, the native Lucayan people called their mysterious island Guanahani. The modern location of Guanahani is believed to be the island now known as San Salvador, although the debate may never entirely be put to rest. What is known is that Columbus departed from that island and landed upon Cuba on October 28, mistakenly thinking it Japan. Undeterred, or blissfully unaware, he pressed onward in his search for China. Adverse winds carried his ships to Haiti and then on to Hispaniola, now known as the Dominican Republic. Fortunately, Columbus had a cartographer with him on the journey, so some sense could be made of the landing points and locations far from the sought-after Asian destination.

Why is this important to the return of the horse to North America? Upon Columbus' return to Spain, King Ferdinand and Queen Isabella recognized the potential of colonization in this newly discovered world. The crown decreed from that point onward that all ships sailing under the Spanish flag would carry horses—*superior horses*. True, land could be explored on foot, a process that offered only a tedious and slow progression. The Spanish Crown had a long-term goal in mind: enrichment and settlement, and probably in that exact order.

Toward that end, horses were shipped with the express purpose of becoming brood stock for subsequent Spanish explorers as the Spaniards sought to establish a toehold on a strange new world.

By royal decree made in Barcelona on May 23, 1493, Ferdinand and Isabella stated:

> Among the persons which we order to go in the . . . armada, we have agreed that twenty lancers, jinetes, are to set sail with horses. Therefore, we mandate that from among the persons of the Holy Brotherhood living in this Kingdom of Granada, the above mentioned twenty horsemen shall be selected. They shall be steadfast and loyal men and

shall sail eagerly. Five of them shall bring spare horses, and those spare horses shall be mares.[3]

It is hardly surprising that human greed came into play. Each of those "steadfast and loyal" men had been provided a specific sum of money to outfit himself for the journey and to purchase a stallion. Five men had been provided with additional funds to procure the five sound breeding mares. The soldiers purchased cheaper stock than, no doubt, the monarchs intended, and promptly pocketed the difference.

On Columbus' second expedition, seventeen ships headed out to the New World with more than one thousand men and twenty-five horses. Those horses were Spanish jennets.

Spanish jennets (sometimes spelled genets) are a type, rather than a breed, of horse. Often descended from Iberian or Barb extraction, they were smaller horses, and they were often gaited. Jennets were considered ideal light horses with good dispositions.

As a point of note, the jennets were carried in stalls and suspended by belly slings for the voyage. Obviously, the long journey to the New World proved terribly hard on the stock, and no doubt deaths occurred en route. The remainder of the initial twenty-five horses disembarked on the island Hispaniola, causing Christopher Columbus to complain in February 1494:

> Concerning the shield-bearers on horseback who came from Granada: in the shoe which they put on in Seville they displayed good horses but later upon departure I did not see them because I was ill. However, they embarked such regrettable beasts on the ship that I do not believe the best one exceeds the value of 2,000 *maravedises* [$300] for they sold the other [horses] and they brought these.[4]

A subset of these "inferior" jennets were transported to Cuba in April 1494. Columbus' orders at the time were not only to establish a permanent colony in the New World, but to create *rancherias* where horses would breed and multiply. On Columbus' third and final voyage in 1498, he returned with fourteen additional mares for that purpose. Four years afterwards in 1502, Nicolas de Ovando received the appointment as the new governor of the Indies, and he arrived with a fleet of thirty ships carrying twenty-five hundred colonists and approximately sixty additional horses. Other explorers and explorations followed, each carrying yet more breeding stock. In a reversal of his earlier decree, in 1507 King Ferdinand banned the exportation of additional equines to the New World for reasons unstated. It seems likely that horses were more in need to expand the Spanish crown's colonization efforts in what is now Morrocco. One thing is for certain: The lack of further equine shipments did not truly matter to the colonies by this point. The Spanish jennet horse population had multiplied, and the horses had once again gained their foothold on the North American continent.

By all accounts, they thrived.

The horse population rapidly expanded in the lush island climate. The Spaniards established many stud farms on the islands, but bureaucrats with a bent toward personal enrichment created laws forbidding export of the valuable mares to new locations. These self-serving laws hindered commerce and created complications for the explorers who required horses for their expeditions. Hernando Cortes found himself tangled in the red tape of these local exportation laws. He also had to fight against inflated prices as he prepared to embark upon a voyage to Mexico in 1518. When the Spanish crown addressed the graft and price gouging, the market fell as the true reality of the situation displayed a horse overpopulation that then drove the market prices down.

Regardless of the economics, in the year 1519 Hernando Cortes led an exploration from Santo Domingo into the interior of Mexico. Driven forward in the quest of seizing fabled riches, colonization and conversion came as secondary motives. Cortes set out with eleven ships, five hundred men, and seventeen horses. They all stepped ashore the Yucatan Peninsula on March 4, 1519, the horses becoming the first equines to actually set foot on the North American continent since prehistoric times. Bernal Diaz de Castillo, a known soldier accompanying Cortes, chronicled the expedition with a particular focus upon the mounts. In his account the *True History of the Conquest of New Spain*, Diaz provided the names, characteristics, and temperaments of individual horses, and to whom the mounts were assigned. The horses, upon reaching solid ground, were allowed to graze for one day before being saddled and armored with breastplates adorned with bells. The purpose of the bells were not intended to locate wandering stock, but instead to terrify the Indigenous inhabitants of the region. In hindsight, it seems doubtful that the bells did much to create terror, but the horses most certainly did.

Thus marks the beginnings of the reintroduction of equines onto the North American landmass. Helpmeets for the Spaniards, the horses had a dual role, acting as weapons of intimidation, conquest, and war.

HORSES RETURN TO THE NORTH AMERICAN LANDMASS

The conquest of Mexico began on the Yucatan Peninsula, where the Spaniards landed on lands inhabited by the Mayan peoples. The local tribes had, understandably, never seen horses before. Terrified by the sight of large beasts carrying armored men, their initial impressions were that man and horse were a type of a centaur—one fantastical being that could decouple at will. While the decoupling part proved accurate, so did the intimidation that ran deep and real for the Mayans. The Spaniards were well aware of the awe their mounted appearance created. In fact, their horses claimed prize of place as a protective asset in warfare. Diaz de Castillo recorded, "the loss of a good horse was more important than that of ten stout men."[5] This sentiment advances the assumption that the Spaniards' horses were well taken care of, and most certainly were kept carefully under guard.

It is important to consider exactly *how* the North American landmass came to be repopulated by horses since it is so vast. Many people adhere to the common, and mistaken, belief that today's wild Mustangs are the direct descendants of the conquistadors' horses. While that assumption is not entirely that far from the truth, the fact is that with one notable exception, Spaniards as a rule *did not ride mares*, but only stallions. One characteristic of the Spanish culture of the sixteenth century was that a conquistador would not *lower* himself to ride a mare—an act that in most contemporaneous views would have proved shameful. The exception to that practice came in the person of Pánfilo de Narváez, who rode a high-spirited and courageous mare despite the prejudice of the time.

Regardless, the suggestion that today's wild horses or Mustangs originate from the Spanish conquistadors' horses comes with attendant problems. The vast majority of those equines landing on the Yucatan Peninsula were, without a doubt, stallions.

Careful mention is made that when Cortes left Mexico with his plunder the first time in 1528, it is recorded that he returned to Spain with his surviving stallions.

Further conquistadors, religious figures, settlers, and their mounts continued to arrive in the New World. The original foundation stock of North American horses began in Central America probably around the year 1514, when it is believed that during the second half of that year, the first mare foaled in the New World.[6] By late 1521, horse breeding at the rancherias took hold and proliferated. The primary aim of those operations was to breed horses for expeditions and conquest. One cannot help coming away with the opinion that while many of the expeditions were mounted, the Spaniards found themselves unsuited for the hostile climate, territory, and inhabitants, whether they were mounted or not.

On April 14, 1528, Narváez arrived in Florida, marking the first-time explorers and their horses set foot onto what would later become the United States of America. He landed with three hundred men and forty horses. Narvaez made the fundamental expedition mistake of allowing his supply ship to travel ahead, never to be seen again. Disastrously, the expedition was unable to ever locate those ships and where they harbored. In time, the unlocated ships returned to Spain, abandoning the men. It is said that Narváez abandoned his horses when he and his men constructed rafts with sails made from the fabric of their shirts. In their desperate attempt to reach a Spanish settlement, more bad luck followed. A storm came up at sea, causing many more men to lose their lives. Seven years later, only four men from the initial expedition survived . . . and remarkably they walked all the way to Mexico City. Narváez was not among the survivors.[7]

That fearsome history did not deter conquistador Hernando de Soto. On May 30, 1539, he and his men landed in Florida, hoping for success where Narváez's expedition had failed. Accompanied by an additional 250 horses (some tally the number at 220, meaning some horses perished en route), de Soto's expedition began near Tampa Bay. In a bizarre twist, a ragged soldier met them on that unknown land. He claimed to have been a member of Narváez's expedition—and since he spoke Spanish and was a Spaniard, that must have been true. This soldier had been taken prisoner by native peoples, and in a quirk of history, the man regaled de Soto with alluring reports of gold and pearls. This dubious report spurred de Soto inland, leading his expedition through what would eventually become Florida, Georgia, the Carolinas, Tennessee, Alabama, Mississippi, Arkansas, Oklahoma, Louisiana, and Texas. Traveling over four thousand miles, this expedition did not fare well either. Unremarkably to modern readers, de Soto and his men failed to locate the gold and pearls that the captive soldier promised. What they found, however, was a lot of untamed land and some rather daunting sights: "While out one day to forage and explore along the beach, de Soto's men came upon an eerie sight: a whole terrain glinting white—not with the sheen of pearls, as they had hoped, but with the bleached bones of Narváez's horses, spread out in the sun."[8]

No further mention is made of the fate of the former captive and his unlikely tale of riches, but one way or another, it must have proved severe.

De Soto rode his favorite stallion Aceituno ("Olive") on this expedition. The horse was killed on the Florida peninsula in a battle (one of many) against native inhabitants, date unknown. Luis de Moscoso Alvarado assumed command of the expedition when de Soto fell ill from fever and died on May 21, 1542, near where Ferriday, Louisiana, is now located. Before his death, de Soto had named Moscoso as the head of the expedition. The expedition sank de Soto's body in the Mississippi River so it would not be disturbed. The remaining men and horses ventured through what is now Texas in the hopes of finding an overland route back to New Spain and civilization. This remnant of de Soto's expedition is credited with bringing the first horses into what would later become known as Texas.

De Soto's expedition (now the Moscoso party), as did so many of the early attempts at exploration and plunder, proved brutal and could be considered a failure from a Spanish perspective. They did not locate any riches or gold for themselves or the crown, but encountered struggle, hardship, and fights with the terrain and the native inhabitants of the

A herd of horses in New Mexico or Arizona between 1899 and 1928.
ARNOLD GENTHE PHOTOGRAPH COLLECTION, LIBRARY OF CONGRESS.

territories. From an equine perspective, the forays proved even worse. In fact, only forty of the horses remained alive three years later due to being consumed for food or having succumbed to disease or hostilities and warfare. One cannot help but imagine the remaining men and their mounts staggering out of a jungle and onto a shore in a desperate attempt to return to the distant coast of Spain.

Of those forty remaining horses belonging to the Moscoso expedition, only twenty-two head remained one year later. Unsurprisingly, the Spaniards decided to abandon their mission. The remaining men and horses set sail for the Gulf of Mexico. To make matters even worse from an equine perspective, along the journey the horses were disembarked for grazing. By this time, word had spread among the Indigenous populations that horses were not immortal, mythical beings. While feeding, the remaining horses were, this time, slaughtered by natives.

Nevertheless, colonization and conquest continued. Exploration also began along the Pacific coastline, near what would become known as Baja Sur, California. European's first contact along the west coast came in the mid-1530s, when Cortez's men ventured into Baja; however, it wouldn't be until late 1770 that the Spaniards pushed north into current Monterey, California, accompanied by horses, livestock, women, and supplies.[9]

FREEDOM OF MOVEMENT

In 1533, a newly issued royal proclamation allowed the public to graze their livestock on communal lands established out of former official parcels. This development permitted greater freedom of equine movement. Under this new decree, the horse populations increased, but more importantly, they formed the basis of free-ranging horses who escaped into the wilds of Mexico.

At the same time, additional rancherias spread into Mexico as well. Antonio de Mendoza, the first viceroy of New Spain (now called Mexico) who arrived in Vera Cruz in late September 1535, is said to have owned at least eleven separate rancherias in Mexico. Horse populations increased throughout the 1530s.

On February 23, 1540, Francisco Vasquez de Coronado began his expedition northward into what is now known as the American Southwest. His route crossed the states of New Mexico, Texas, Oklahoma, Kansas, and Arizona. He acquired hundreds of horses and mules for the journey, expecting to bring back a plethora of gold and treasure. Though that treasure did not exist. Pedro de Casteneda, a chronicler of the expedition, states that they started with one thousand horses and six hundred pack animals, while Coronado himself claimed the number to be fifteen hundred horses and mules. Whatever the tally, it is likely that a few horses managed to escape from poorly or hastily built corrals. Once again assuming most (if not all) were stallions and likely without breeding mares, the horses' ability to reproduce remained limited.

Even if the escaped horses did not breed, their existence in the wild allowed Indigenious tribes to familiarize themselves with the animals.

As for Coronado's expedition, that familiarity remained in the future. The Pueblo Indians killed sixty of Coronado's mounts in present-day New Mexico. In April 1542 disheartened and with both men and horses starving and dying from disease and winter hardships, Coronado's expedition retreated southward to the comparative safety of Mexico.[10]

Inland, the Spaniards, chastened by their experiences, did not return to what is now the United States for thirty-nine years, arriving in 1581, when priests Augustin Rodrigues, Francisco Lopez, and Juan de Santa, along with nine soldiers, nineteen Indian servants, six hundred head of stock, and ninety horses made their way north into what is now New Mexico.[11] This time, it is believed that mares accompanied the rest of the livestock. This is also a possible event marking the beginning of the Mustang horse north of Mexico.

The Spanish colonization of the New World marched on with the strong likelihood that Juan de Onate and his colonists from New Spain (Mexico) introduced horse breeding into the southwestern United States. Onate brought twenty-five stallions, fifty-five mares, and some foals. On April 30, 1598, he led his party along the middle of the Rio Grande River into what would become New Mexico. In July 1598, Onate met with the leaders of thirty-one pueblos at the Santo Domingo pueblo. According to the Spaniards, all agreed to become subjects of the king of Spain.

Riding on that success, Onate was appointed as the colonial governor of Santa Fe in November of 1598, and his allotment of horses was increased to eight hundred. Those eight hundred head signaled a notable increase in wealth and prestige.

The seeds of discontent and distrust, however, were sowed among the Pueblo peoples.

Any doubts the Puebloes entertained about Spanish rule came to bloody fruition. In 1599, a massacre of approximately eight hundred people occurred at the Acoma Pueblo in retaliation for the killing of twelve Spaniards. The Acoma who survived the clash faced horrific punishments—some twenty-four suffered punitive amputations while others suffered twenty years of enslavement. During their enslavement, some of them must have come into contact with the horses and learned of their uses and care. The massacre and its aftermath, for understandable reasons, lingered in the Acoma and Puebloan people's memory and festered. This hostility remained against Spanish "rule" for eighty-one more years.

Meanwhile, "Alta California" remained on the fringes of the Spanish empire until 1769 when a "sacred mission" led by Captain Gaspar de Portola and Franciscan friar Junipero Serra established outposts in San

Diego and Monterrey. Despite numerous failed attempts by sea beginning in the mid-1530s when Cortez's men ventured to Baja California, it wasn't until 1542 that Spaniards sailed north to Alta California. Juan Rodriguez Cabrillo's expedition that year made landings as far north as modern Santa Barbara. Waiting over two hundred more years, the Spaniards again set northward from Baja California and progressed as far as San Diego in 1769. Eventually, they crossed the low mountains and pressed further north along the Pacific coast where they established a settlement in Monterey in 1770, establishing the beginnings of the mission culture. This is the point when it is largely assumed that horses arrived on the western coastline of the United States.[12]

The last herds of any size to "seed" Alta California arrived in 1774 when Juan Bautista de Anza traveled from Sonora and wound his way through Arizona's Yuma Territory, crossing the San Carlos Pass of the Sierra Nevada and arrived in the San Francisco area on October 25, 1775, with seven hundred horses (and cattle, of course) bred in Arizona's Tubac Presidio, established in 1752, near present-day Tucson. The Presidio, established to protect settlers against the Apache and other tribes, was manned by a cavalry of Spanish soldiers, effectively making them the first established cavalry west of the Mississippi.[13]

Although California is considered a comparative latecomer in the history of the reintroduction of equines to the North American landmass, it nevertheless played an important role.

Western Horse Trivia

The "Horse Latitudes" in the Atlantic Ocean gained its name from the sad fact that innumerable dead horses were thrown overboard into the ocean during early voyages of colonization. Records from the 1800s tell of the frequent death of valuable horses, lost to the stormy Atlantic.[14]

NOTES

1. Deb Bennett, *Conquerors: The Roots of New World Horsemanship*, Solvang, CA: Amigo Publications, 1998, 4.

2. "From Waterhole to Rhino Barn," https://ashfall.unl.edu/about-ashfall/waterhole-to-rhino-barn.html.

3. Bennett, *Conquerors*, 152.

4. Bennett, *Conquerors*, 152.

5. Bernal Diaz del Castillo, *True History of the Conquest of New Spain*, 1632, https://www.gutenberg.org/files/32474/32474-h/32474-h.htm. Note: Diaz del Castillo died in 1584, so this account was published posthumously but is considered the seminal work of the Spanish conquest.

6. Bennett, *Conquerors*, 183.

7. "The Misadventures of Pánfilo Narváez and Nuñez de Cabeza de Vaca," https://fcit.usf.edu/florida/lessons/narvaez/narvaez1.htm#:~:text=Pánfilo%20de%20Narváez%20arrived%20near,he%20was%20able%20to%20control.

8. Bennett, *Conquerors*, 304.

9. Library of Congress, "California as I Saw It: First-Person Narratives of California's Early Years, 1849 to 1900," https://www.loc.gov/collections/california-first-person-narratives/articles-and-essays/early-california-history.

10. Dennis Herrick, "Xauian and the Tiguex War," *Native Peoples Magazine*, January/February 2014, http://dennisherrick.com/Xau%C3%ADan.

11. Agapito Rey, "The Rodriguez Expedition to New Mexico 1581–1582," original publication 1927, *New Mexico Historical Review* 2, 3 (1927): article 3, https://digitalrepository.unm.edu/cgi/viewcontent.cgi?article=1405&context=nmhr.

12. Library of Congress, "California as I Saw It."

13. Charles R. Eatherly, "Opened and Dedicated September 28, 1958," https://azstateparks.com/tubac/about-the-presidio/park-history.

14. "The Spanish Returns Equus to its Prehistoric Homes—The Perilous Crossing," https://imh.org/exhibits/past/legacy-of-the-horse/spanish-return-equus-its-prehistoric-home.

CHAPTER 2

THE HORSE AND THE AMERICAN INDIAN, BEFORE 1860

Two Salish women in their finery—but notice the horses and their finery.
CHARLES E. SIMMONS (LIBRARY OF CONGRESS)

EXCITING RECENT SCHOLARSHIP, BASED UPON INDIGENOUS ORAL HIS-
tory and confirmed by archaeology, presents evidence that horses
migrated northward independent from the Spanish explorers. True, the
equines were offspring of the Spanish imports. However, this new scholarship backs tribal claims that some Indigenous populations have owned,
or at least have been aware of, horses prior to the Europeans' arrival in

the western United States. Recent scientific findings now support these oral histories. They posit:

> These [traditionally accepted] records, made a century after the revolt, do not align with the oral histories of the Comanche and Shoshone people, who document horse use far earlier. Using tools such as radiocarbon dating, ancient and modern DNA analysis and isotope analysis (isotopes are elements with varying numbers of neutrons in their nuclei), a large and diverse team of researchers from 15 countries and multiple Native American groups, including members of the Lakota, Comanche and Pawnee nations, have now determined that horses did indeed spread across the continent earlier and faster than previously assumed. . . . The team discovered that two horses—one from Paa'ko Pueblo, New Mexico, and one from American Falls, Idaho—dated from the early 1600s, decades before Spanish settlers arrived in that area. By 1650, horses abounded in the Southwest and Great Plains, the researchers found.[1]

According to archaeological evidence, the newly studied horse remains display evidence of care and display markings on their teeth that signify a type of bridle usage. The use of bridles implies that those early horses were, in fact, controlled and ridden. The size of those earliest horse herds were, as of this writing, yet unknown and unquantified. However, these accounts also fall in line with Ute oral history. Tribal historians record that the Mouache band (eastern Ute) acquired horses from the Spanish in 1580, and that the Ute as a people owned horses by 1637, which would make them the first Native Americans to assimilate the horse culture.

This adds a new dimension to a commonly accepted history that may end up transformational in the study of the expansion of the horse through the American West.

In mostearlier scholarship, the Pueblo Revolt of 1680 historically marked the "dispersal" of horses into the wilderness of that region. A reprisal against the repressive Spanish colonization, the Pueblo people drove the Spaniards from the region, and in their haste, they left many of their possessions, including livestock, behind as they fled. As noted previously, many accounts claim that the Pueblo people (the victors of the revolt) were ambivalent toward their newly captured horses. In fact, they were seen as large "nuisances" who apparently roamed at will and trampled and ate the Pueblos' crops. In short, the horses did not exactly "take" in their life and culture. That said, the Pueblo people realized that the horses had value.

They could be traded to other tribes.

LEARNING ABOUT HORSES

Historically, the Spaniards certainly did not want American Indians to have access to, or use of, horses. For both subjugation and security purposes, the Spanish explorers and first settlers refused to teach the local Indigenous peoples how to ride. Slaves or peons were allowed, no doubt, to care for the equines and to work near and around them, but mastery of riding remained forbidden. It escaped no one's notice, if they stopped to think about it, and certainly they must have, that stallions, mares, and their offspring conveyed status to their owners. Horses were a *useful* wealth, and most would argue of primary importance in the expansive western region of the United States. The horses offered a freedom of movement previously unknown to Indigenous people. Large amounts of territory could be covered with comparatively little effort on the part of humans. The Spaniards certainly wanted to avoid the complications and repercussions that mounted tribes would surely present.

Mounted enemies were not so easily subjugated as those on foot. Horse ownership and mastery conferred a measure of equality economically, offensively, and defensively. A man seated upon a large horse was a man seated upon a large horse no matter the race or nationality. Horses could be used for war, transportation, and labor, all the while implying a real measure of wealth and status.

HORSE DISPERSAL IN THE SOUTHWEST

Using the traditional starting point of the Pueblo Uprising in 1680 for the sake of clarity, there is no real question that the Spaniards' herd dispersal throughout the region occurred during and after the rebellion. This momentous upheaval transpired under the auspices of Po'pay (or Popé in Spanish), a Tewa religious leader from the San Juan Pueblo in August of 1680. Within three days of the uprising, all the Spanish settlements, with the exception of Santa Fe, lay in ruins. The overriding desire of the victorious Puebloans was to erase any and all traces of the Spaniards and to reclaim their land and autonomy. In short, they wanted to restore their lives and world to what they had been before the colonization. As mentioned, during the Spaniards' haste to flee in the face of the onslaught, they abandoned both livestock and horses. The victorious Pueblo people traded the "nuisance" Spaniards' horses to other nearby tribes, widening the horse "frontier" from New Mexico into, and among, the neighboring regions and peoples. Whether those horses were traded first to the Apache or Comanche is impossible to pinpoint exactly. Trade routes, nevertheless, were established from New Mexico, up across the Colorado Plateau, to the Rocky Mountains, and into the Great Plains. By the 1730s, horses spread westward into the northwestern plains of what are now the states of Oregon and Washington.

Once again, a fair amount of speculation is required to pinpoint the exact details as to how horse trading and dissemination took place. Tribes had already established interconnections and trade routes over time. And if a particular tribe preferred to act as a broker, rather than owning horses themselves, brokering tribes were happy to act as middlemen. Such was the case with the Brule Lakota. The Omaha Nation loved their horses, but they were also happy to trade, or sell, them. The Brule Lakota acquired the horse from Omaha Indian traders in 1708.[2]

In short, the introduction of the horse to the American Indians changed almost everything.

Many of the Indigenous people marked time as before and after the horse. "Equestrian nomads," it was quickly discovered, "could do almost everything—move, hunt, trade, fight, kill, evade, and protect themselves—faster and more efficiently."[3] Equines also shifted the balance of power among tribes. The nations that quickly embraced and mastered the uses of the horse could capitalize on the attendant advantages over the other nations who proved slower to adopt.

The Southern Range

It stands to reason that those nations nearest in proximity to the Spanish settlements were the first to master the usage of the equines. Around the year 1700, the Utes, Comanches, Shoshones, and Apaches controlled a large swath of land west of the current state of New Mexico, which ranged northward into the present states of Utah and Colorado. The Utes, who were related to the Shoshone (a tribe farther north) and Comanche peoples, entered into an alliance whereby they shared their land, horses, and guns. The Comanche Tribe, who called themselves the *numunuu*, split off from their Shoshone kin in the late 1600s or early 1700s and headed farther into the southern plains. The reason for the split is unclear, but it illustrates that tribal dynamics played a role in Indigenous history and movement as well.

Within a relatively short period of time, this alliance actively raided in New Mexico seeking yet more horses . . . and captives.

Likewise, in the seventeenth century, the Apache range or territory was located farther north. Quick to realize the horses' value, by the 1650s they are believed to have been a serious mounted force. Once again, the routes and handoffs become a bit clouded at this point, but scholarship exists suggesting that horses acquired prior to the Spanish arrival traveled via trade routes stemming from northern Mexico. Those trade routes were used and controlled by a people known as the Jumanos, who occupied areas in the Texas Plains.[4] The Jumanos people themselves have become an enigma, but it is believed that slavery and warfare took its toll. In time, the Apaches would partially absorb and partially annihilate the Jumanos. What is known is that the Jumanos are no longer a distinct people claiming that identity.

During that same approximate time frame, the northern Comanches swept down from the Arkansas River Valley of the Southern Rocky Mountains, after having learned horsemanship from their allies the Utes. In fact, the name Comanche is probably derived from a Southern Ute term meaning "stranger." By the 1710s, the Comanche (as a people) had enough horses to hunt the southern plains bison. The Apaches, at this time, were semi-nomadic, and although mounted and owning horses, they also farmed along the rivers. The Comanches, who remained a purely nomadic people, swept them aside from the southern plains and pushed them into the western margins. During the 1760s, the Kiowas inhabited the northern great plains but attached themselves to the Comanche trade routes. In the 1780s, drawn to the southern climate and greater horse prosperity and wealth, the Kiowa moved southward, where they clashed with the Comanche.

Much of this vast and widespread territorial movement came with the introduction of the horse.

In 1806, the Comanche and the Kiowa made peace and became lasting allies. Once the Kiowa moved south, a void remained where they had formerly lived, and the Cheyenne and Arapahoe migrated from the northern Black Hills down near the Mandan-Hidatsa trade crossroads along the central Missouri River. The Cheyenne and Arapahoe became intermediaries (as well as superb horsemen) and conducted trade in the current Colorado area, Bent's Fort in specific. Trade became established in the 1830s but ended in 1849 during the great cholera epidemic. The Cheyenne and Arapahoe firmly established themselves as northern links in the horse-trading chain.

New rivalries emerged as the horses spread, as did economic and sovereign opportunities. Mounted raiding parties could travel further with comparative ease. European weaponry became a much-sought commodity as "raids, retaliations, retreats, and expansions settled into a brutal and draining cycle."[5] Horses offered yet another means of barter: trading for goods and weapons. Horse raiding became almost a sport and flourished among such tribes as the Sioux, Blackfeet, Crow, Cheyenne, and other nomadic peoples. Becoming a mounted culture allowed tribes to expand territories and claim lands belonging to weaker tribes and peoples.

Cultures of various nations, tribes, and bands changed due to their adoption of the horse. Semi-nomadic peoples, such as the Pawnees, often chose to act as brokers, whereas the Lakota, who were comparative newcomers from the east, embraced what would become the Great Plains horse culture. Prior to their arrival west, they were semi-nomadic and weaker than neighboring tribes.

Ousted by peoples in the Great Lakes region such as the Ojibway, Saux, Fox, Iowas, Arikaras, and more, the Lakota forged a new identity for themselves, and that identity revolved around the horse. The Lakota, who illustrated historically important events on painted hides called *winter counts*, depicted attacks by tribes who visually owned more horses, brandished weapons including guns, and were aligned with greater numbers of allies. By the 1760s, the Lakota advanced along the Missouri River and their winter count depictions began to change.

Horses were traded even further into the north via the Rio Grande Valley and the Rocky Mountains. The Shoshone and Flatheads obtained horses by 1700, and Crow and Blackfeet had them by 1740. By the 1750s, horses existed in all regions of the plains. In the 1780s, the Lakotas had acquired enough horses via raids or trading with the Arikara to establish themselves as an equestrian force that equaled the Comanche to the south.

That change illustrates how horses changed the balance of power.

CALIFORNIA AND THE NORTHWEST REGION

The horse population came a bit later to the American Northwest, but by the year 1730 there is record of mounted Shoshone fighting against the Piegans—a Blackfoot tribal relative in what is now Canada and Montana. The Piegans initially referred to the horse, which they had never seen before, as "Elk Dogs."[6]

Now that many of the tribes were mounted, the next acquisition desired was better weaponry. During the eighteenth century, guns were traded with the tribes in the east and in the trading posts of the west and Pacific Northwest. The southern plains people had access to goods and weapons traveling along the Santa Fe Trail established in 1822.

Again, some Great Lakes regional tribes such as the already mentioned Lakota Sioux, the Cheyenne, and the Crow were forced out from that region and onto the Great Plains by better armed tribes, such as the Ojibway. They were armed in 1745 as British and French trading posts were established in that region during the seventeenth and eighteenth centuries.

As an afterthought, an argument might be made that the well-armed tribes did not "take" as strongly to the mounted way of life. Horses became an integral part of the cultures of the then-weaker Sioux, Cheyenne, Crow, Comanche, Ute, Nez Perce, and Blackfeet, among others.

In the "horse tribes" of the West, the horse as a being rose to a place of prominence and high regard. Both on a practical and spiritual plane.

AMERICAN INDIAN HORSE CULTURE

Horses quickly obtained prominence in the cultures that adopted them, nearing mythical status and exalted standing. In many instances, horses were treated as kin and were honored as such.

Horse societies formed, as did the expanded practice of counting coup by stealing war horses staked near enemy tribes' teepees. *Counting coup* refers to the practice of striking an enemy without causing death, symbolizing great bravery. Conversely, counting coup also amounted to a means of dishonoring or discounting the enemy by touching him. A widespread belief was held that in striking the enemy warrior, some of

Lassoing Wild Horses by W. W. Rice (active 1846–1860).
LIBRARY OF CONGRESS.

his strength and courage would transfer to the man who counted coup. This practice began while the tribes were still on foot, in hand-to-hand combat. The practice and possibility of counting coup grew exponentially with the introduction of the horse.

Although the origins of counting coup come from the past, modern instances still exist. There is the most remarkable account given by Joe Medicine Crow (a member of the Crow Nation) who served during World War II. In Germany, on one occasion he overpowered and disarmed a German soldier in hand-to-hand combat. He went on to later steal horses from an SS unit, whom they captured as well. The tribal elders, upon his return to Montana, determined that Joe's actions qualified as counting coup. In addition, for his bravery during World War II, he received a Bronze Star, the French Chevalier de la Légion d'Honneur medal, and the Presidential Medal of Freedom awarded by President Barack Obama.[7]

HORSES AS ART AND THEIR OWN DECORATION

Horses were depicted in many forms of art, ranging from winter counts to paintings on hides and tipis, not to mention breathtaking and fabulous beadwork. The horses themselves, like the warriors who rode them, were often decorated with paint. It is next to impossible to describe the feelings upon seeing a live horse painted with tribal markings in the modern day. The horses stand a bit prouder and taller in their warpaint. They look very proud of themselves—and well they should!

Historically, horses were decorated with symbols and medicine paint to intimidate the enemy, to bolster the horses' confidence and courage in battle, and to record the achievements of both horse and rider. Imbued with mystical, indeed almost magical, meanings in many instances, a circle painted around a horse's eye allowed the horse better vision, and likewise a circle around the nostril represented enhanced ability to smell. Handprints placed on the horse could count the number of enemies killed in hand-to-hand combat without weapons. A handprint specifically on the shoulder meant an oath of vengeance. Coup marks were often straight lines (like notches on a gun) that symbolized the times the horse and rider were in battles or enemy camps. Hail marks (small circles) symbolized the desire for a horse and rider to fall upon the enemy like hail. The horse might also be decorated with thunder or lightning bolts to symbolize speed or power, and hoofprints symbolized the number of times the horse and rider had successfully stolen horses from the enemy. Straight arrows symbolized victory, and broken arrows (or fire arrows) portrayed the hope for bad luck for the enemy.

Made from natural pigments blended with animal fat or water, colors available depended upon the natural resources close at hand. Ashes made gray and white, charcoal made black, berries made anywhere from red to blue colors dependent upon the variety, and ocher (yellow iron oxide) made yellow.

On many occasions, a warrior and his horse wore matching painted symbols.

Beyond painting, horses' manes were often symbolically decorated. Items such as a lock of the rider's hair woven into the mane symbolized unity or kinship between the horse and the rider. Feathers bound to the mane were meant to lend the horse the speed and agility of a bird.

HORSES AS SPORT AND A MEANS OF OBTAINING WEALTH

Horse raiding was a popular way to bolster tribal herd sizes and increase economic wealth of the tribes (and specifically the raiders) who stole or captured the horses. There was also a strong element of sport in the raider's prowess. One interesting fact of the horse raiding and the tribal ownership cultures: Brave victors often gave away horses as signs of respect and generosity, as well as a means of emphasizing their bravery. Some chiefs and war chiefs owned immense herds numbering in the hundreds or even thousands.

Most tribes did not corral or contain their horses with one exception: the war horse or the war pony. As noted earlier, one way of showing bravery was stealing horses hobbled near a warrior's tipi—these would be the war horses. In fact, warriors rode horses, although Europeans often referred to them as ponies due to their smaller stature. Regardless, a man's war horse was more than just a possession—the relationship ran deep. A war horse was a partner, a brother, a friend. In fact, in severely inclement weather, it is said that warriors might go as far as to bring their war horse into their lodge, telling their wife and children to find somewhere else to shelter.

War ponies were trained by their riders over several years. Battle was no place for an unreliable mount. In fact, "it has been said that most frequent argument between a horseman and his wife was over the war pony.[8]

For those horses of lesser status, the "non-war-horse" equines, young boys often guarded the herds at night.

Tribes had tack for their horses such as leather or woven hair harnesses tied around the horses' bottom jaw where the natural gap in their teeth occurs. Today, these woven hair harnesses used as lower jaw bridles are often referred to as "war bridles." The horses, as prized possessions and bona fide members of the family, were often richly decorated in fabulous beaded, quilled, or painted horse blankets, pads, and saddles. Some of those saddles had pommels and cantles (horns and the back of seats for stability) and perhaps a device to hang a cradleboard. Many of the saddles had stirrups, which makes sense from a stability perspective. Made of wood and/or rawhide, in ledger paintings and decorations those saddles and stirrups are often omitted. Antique staged photographs also show warriors in all their splendor seated atop their horses using blankets or pads, perhaps posing simply for the photograph.

Quirts, used to urge horses to run faster, could be works of art as well, as were special sticks for counting coup. Some tribes also used horse masks for their mounts—decorated rawhide or canvas that were crafted with fine and fabulous skill.

AMERICAN HORSE BREEDS AND AMERICAN INDIAN STOCK

In 1803, the United States embarked into a transaction with France whereby it purchased 828,000 square miles of land west of the Mississippi River for fifteen million dollars, which equated to roughly four cents an acre. The fledgling nation expanded westward—and found mounted American Indians and a flourishing horse culture.

By 1850, it was estimated that more than two million descendants of those Spanish horses roamed throughout the American West. Mustangs were the foundation of the western American horse. The name "Mustang" originates from the Mexican Spanish word *mestego*, which means "animal that strays." From the Mustang came the fabulous Appaloosa horses associated with the Nez Perce Tribe in the American Northwest. The name Appaloosa may come from "a Palouse," referring to the region where the horses were bred in Washington and Idaho in a location proximate to the Palouse River.[9] The Appaloosa were the descendants of Spanish spotted horses, a marking or pattern favored by the Nez Perce. Lewis and Clark made favorable note of the spotted horses on their historic expedition.

Cayuse, or full name Cayuse Indian Pony, was a small and stocky horse that reportedly had become a distinct breed by the nineteenth century. Named for the Cayuse people of eastern Washington and Oregon, they are thought to have been descended, in part, from Spanish Barb horses and Percherons. "The breed's history is obscure and difficult to trace. It has been generally accepted that the Cayuse Indian Pony descended from the French-Norman horses imported into Canada in the 1600s. Most of these French horses were Percherons, which the Canadians used to improve their domestic breeds."[10] By the 1800s, the Cayuse developed into a separate breed. "The Cayuse Indians, known throughout the Northwest for their expert horsemanship, continued to develop this French-Spanish Barb strain through selective breeding. Because the Percheron had the ability to pass on its tendency for spots or a profusion of white markings, the Cayuse people were able to produce some very colorful horses. In fact, the Appaloosa, Paint and Pinto breeds have all been influenced by the blood of the Cayuse Indian Pony."[11]

In the twenty-first century, the breed has declined and has become relatively rare.

Historically, both Paint and Pinto breeds are descendants of the Spanish stock, meaning Mustangs. Paints and Pintos were loved by cowboys and revered by many American Indian tribes who believed the horses possessed magical powers. They have great working ability and a willing attitude. Pintos are a color breed and can be of any genetic ancestry, while Paints must be registered with the American Paint Horse or other specific associations to be qualified as a true Paint. Back in the 1800s, this distinction was not made.

Tribes, such as the Nez Perce and the Cayuse, bred horses to display special characteristics. The Nez Perce (formerly of the Palouse Tribe) bred Appaloosas (first called a Palouse Horse), preferring the spotted coats. Over time, lore has it that the name changed from *a Palouse* horse to an *Appaloosa*. The Nez Perce were skillful breeders, gelding males that they felt were below their exacting standards and trading off females they deemed unsuitable. This breed of horse was nearly obliterated between 1876 and 1877 as the US Army seized tribal lands. There are five main coat patterns recognized in this breed: Leopard is characterized by a white coat over most or all of the body with dark egg or rounded shapes on the white; snowflake is where white spotting occurs all over the body, concentrated on the hips; blanket is where the coat color over the hips can be either white or spotted; marbleized, where there is a mottled pattern all over the body; and frost, which consists of white specks on a dark coat.

The Cayuse, who lived near the Nez Perce, may have discovered their horses from stock turned away by the Nez Perce breeders. The Cayuse have lived on the Umatilla Indian Reservation since 1855. White settlers for a time referred to all horses that belonged to American Indians as "Cayuse," but the Cayuse Indian Pony is a distinct breed probably originating in the 1800s. Although the Cayuse Pony's ancestry is unclear, they may be descended from Percherons that were imported into Canada. This breed could be any color. The Cayuse people practiced selective breeding, probably crossing the Percherons with the lighter Spanish Barbs.[12] The Cayuse horses were famed for their speed and endurance and would be later sought by the Pony Express.

The Cayuse Pony was said to be superior to the large US Cavalry horses, although that probably depended upon the specific horses in question.

Tribal Horses

Historical references recorded by Europeans concerning the tribal horses are usually glowing.

The War Party (Crow Nation).
EDWARD CURTIS. LIBRARY OF CONGRESS.

The "noble Cheyenne" had, as the author obviously expected, noble horses. Alexander Henry came upon them in 1806, south of the Missouri River during a gala occasion. "Their horses," he recorded,

> were mostly beautiful, spirited beasts; some were masked in a very singular manner, to imitate the head of a buffalo, red deer, or cabbrie [sic—and meaning a ruminant animal of the desert plains—possibly a mountain goat or antelope?], with horns, the mouth and nostrils—even the eyes—trimmed with red cloth. They were by far the best built and most active horses I have seen in this country—superior in every respect to those we see northward. The first great war chief was mounted on a handsome black stallion.[13]

Thomas James was an early western mountain man and horse trader who dealt with the Comanche and the Utes. In 1823, he made an expedition among them and wrote a book about his experiences titled *Three Years Among the Indians and the Mexicans*, published in 1827. In that account, he focuses a great deal upon their mounts. On the Canadian River in present-day Texas, James traded for seventeen "really fine animals worth at least $100 in St. Louis." His price? Approximately ten dollars' worth of calico, tobacco, knives, mirrors, and other trinkets per each horse purchased. If he did not exaggerate, that would leave a profit of ninety dollars per horse. That said, however, one would have to get them back to St. Louis, which would prove no easy feat. Regardless of the economics, James' trading continued until he had assembled 323 horses. Although the origins of those horses are unclear as to whether they were all obtained from the Comanche, in Santa Fe he records how Ute warriors came to him. "They came riding into the city and paraded on the public square, all well mounted on the most elegant horses I have ever seen, animals of a superior breed, with slender, tapering legs and short, fine hair, like pure best blooded races, some spotted and striped as if painted for ornament."[14] Apparently, he must have bought some. On James' return to St. Louis with his equine prizes, he experienced stampedes and other horses dying from horsefly bites.

Renowned artist George Catlin also heard tales and descriptions of Comanche horsemanship and their majestic herds. In 1834 and 1835, he recorded what he saw in a famous painting titled *Comanche Feats of Horsemanship*. Catlin considered the Comanche as superior to the Sioux or the northern tribes he had studied and painted. As Dobie records, with the Comanche he found "at least 3,000 horses and mules. . . . Although there were some tolerable nags amongst this medley group of all colors and shapes," the horses were, he found, "generally small of the wild breed, tough and serviceable."[15]

He also recorded that perhaps a third of the count were mules, which he claimed as "more valuable than horses."[16]

Some of the bands and tribes on the plains amassed huge horse herds. As the West became increasingly contested, those horses, while proving an asset in battles and skirmishes, also became a form of collateral damage. The Red River Wars and the massacre at Palo Duro Canyon in the Texas Panhandle is one such travesty. The battle occurred on September 28, 1874. Comanche, Southern Cheyenne, Arapaho, and Kiowa warriors, led by Lone Wolf, left their respective reservations and gathered in the Palo Duro Canyon. The US Army, led by Ranald S. Mackenzie, discovered the warriors, and a battle ensued. It was estimated that the warriors held about two thousand horses. Some horses fled with the warriors out onto the plains; however, the remaining horses were rounded up. Those not claimed by officers or soldiers (it is assumed about 340 horses were claimed) were literally gunned down to prevent them from returning into the warriors' hands.

Without their horses, several tribes could not hold out over the winter and returned to captivity in Fort Sill by November 1874.[17]

The loss of all those horses hurts the heart.

THE NEZ PERCE

No other tribe was as closely associated with a specific breed as the Nez Perce and their horses. The Nez Perce agreed, in 1855, to a large reservation with the US government via treaty. The land encompassed most of their traditional territory along the lower Snake River and in the basins of the Salmon and Clearwater Rivers. Unfortunately, in 1860, gold was discovered in the Clearwater region of Idaho.

Rich placer diggings sprung up on the reservation, heedless of trespassing. Thousands of prospectors and homesteaders flowed in, and the US government forcibly "renegotiated" the treaty in 1863, decreasing the tribal land by three-fourths of the original reservation size. Still, the encroachment continued, and the European settlers wanted yet more. The Nez Perce, perhaps most of their tribal members, had never agreed to either treaty. By 1870, homesteaders had settled along the reservation boundaries, and preferring to pasture their stock on the unfenced range, encroached on tribal lands. The settlers complained of the Nez Perce stallions on the range, assuming the Appaloosas as inferior stock to their large and heavy-boned New England horses.

About this time, a new Indian agent named John Monteith was assigned to the Nez Perce reservation. He disapproved of the Nez Perce (or any Indigenous peoples) raising horses for the simple economic reason that sales of their horses provided the tribes with economic independence. He felt that was to be avoided at all costs. Tribal members could sell horses to miners, homesteaders, or anyone who needed a mount. Obviously, a means of making money lessened their dependence on the government. Additionally, if governmental regulation became viewed as too troublesome, horses allowed the Nez Perce to move to other locations away from interference.[18]

As a result, in 1877 Monteith sought use of the cavalry to force all non-treaty Nez Perce onto the reservation. One of the richest and the largest bands was led by Chief Joseph and was known as the Wallowa Band. They held a herd of horses numbering in the thousands, which they pastured between Wallowa Mountain Range and the Snake River Canyon in Oregon. When they received word to come into the reservation, they fled instead of complying with the summons. When the band crossed the torrent of the Snake River Canyon, about nine hundred horses were lost. It is unknown whether those horses drowned or simply did not make the crossing. Four young braves from the Salmon River Band killed four settlers in revenge, thus sparking off what is now known as the Nez Perce War.

Because the war broke quickly, many of the Appaloosas were still out on the range. Treated, in this instance, as the spoils of war, they were claimed by the first people who could corral them. The Nez Perce horses were often sold to western cattlemen and bred with other horses. The Appaloosas became a "lost breed," with their history neglected until 1937. True, the Nez Perce still bred their horses, but on the reservation. It took publicity, including an article that came out in January 1937 in *Western Horseman* entitled "The Appaloosa, or Palouse Horse," to result in the Appaloosa Horse Club being established in 1938.[19]

Western Horse Trivia

The Ute Tribe often trained their horses by mounting them in rivers. That way if the rider was thrown, the landing was softer.

NOTES

1. Kristina Kilgrove, "Indigenous People of the American West Used 'Sacred' Horses a Half Century Earlier than Previously Thought," *Live Science* (March 30, 2023), https://www.livescience.com/indigenous-people-of-the-american-west-used-sacred-horses-a-half-century-earlier-than-previously-thought.

2. Pekka Hämäläinen, *Lakota America: A New Indigenous Power*, New Haven, CT: Yale University Press, 2019, 50.

3. Pekka Hämäläinen, *Indigenous Continent: The Epic Contest for North America*, New York, NY: Liveright Publishing Corporation, 2022, 250–52.

4. Pekka Hämäläinen, "The Rise and Fall of Plains Indian Horse Cultures," *History Cooperative*, https://historycooperative.org/journal/the-rise-and-fall-of-plains-indian -horse-cultures.

5. Hämäläinen, "The Rise and Fall of Plains Indian Horse Cultures."

6. American Indian Partnership. Blackfeet Timeline, http://www .americanindianpartnership.com/blackfeet-timeline.html.

7. Joseph Medicine Crow, *Counting Coup: Becoming a Crow Chief on the Reservation and Beyond*, Washington, DC: National Geographic, 2003, 107–17.

8. Gawani Pony Boy, *Horse Follow Closely: Native American Horsemanship*, Irvine, CA: Bow Tie Press, 1998, 9.

9. Appaloosa Museum. "History of the Appaloosa," http://www.appaloosamuseum .com/history-of-the-appaloosa.

10. Rachel Berry, "Breed of Livestock—Cayuse Indian Pony," http://afs.okstate.edu/ breeds/horses/cayuseindian/index.html.

11. Berry, "Breed of Livestock—Cayuse Indian Pony."

12. Elwyn Hartley Edwards, *The Horse Encyclopedia*, London, England: DK Publishing, 2016, 314.

13. Gen. Thomas James, *Three Years Among the Indians and the Mexicans*, St. Louis, MO: Missouri Historical Society, MCMXVI, 202.

14. James, *Three Years Among the Indians*, 144.

15. J. Frank Dobie, *The Mustangs*, Edison, NJ: Castle Books, 1952, 72.

16. Dobie, *The Mustangs*, 234.

17. Thomas F. Schilz, "Battle of Palo Duro Canyon," Texas State Historical Association, August 4, 2020, https://www.tshaonline.org/handbook/entries/palo-duro-canyon -battle-of.

18. Frances Haines, *Appaloosa: The Spotted Horse in Art and History*, Austin, TX: University of Texas Press, 91.

19. Haines, *Appaloosa*, 98.

CHAPTER 3

THE CAVALRY, 1861-1900

THE US CAVALRY, DRESSED IN DEEP UNIFORM BLUE, MOUNTED ON FINE steeds upon bluffs overlooking a hostile territory beyond, is seared into the imagination of anyone whoever watches, or has watched, western movies. That the cavalry rode to the rescue of beleaguered parties and saved the day is another stereotypical notion many hold dear. But that heroic vision paints a picture that only marginally existed. The life of a cavalryman or infantry soldier was full of deprivations. That glorious story of charging steeds and running battles did exist—but the outcomes were never entirely certain. Especially not for the individual or his mount. It was a hard existence to man outposts in the West. As a rule, the attention focuses on the men, rather than on their indispensable mounts, those magnificent horses who carried the day or suffered right alongside their riders.

To begin, the term (or word) *cavalry* comes from the French word *cavalerie* dating from the 1590s, or the Italian *cavalleria* which can mean either mounted soldier or knight, or a gentleman who serves as a lady's escort.[1]

European roots aside, the US Cavalry traces its origins back to 1832. Precipitating their creation, in 1831, a series of engagements and battles known as the Black Hawk War broke out. This war combined elements of intertribal hostilities and duplicity, along with more dishonesty and the encroachment of white settlement onto the Sauks' traditional hunting grounds and territory. This series of conflicts also served as a precursor of the future to come regarding American Indian and white clashes, but also highlighted a critical lack. When American officials decided to force Black Hawk's band out of the region, General Edmund P. Gaines, the commander of the Western Department of the US Army, had no mounted troops with which to pursue the mounted Sauk warriors.

It is remarkable that the Sauks and their allies had horses, but the US Army did not . . . beyond heavy supply horses and perhaps some officers' private mounts.

The tribal warriors on horseback were far more mobile, and the US Army found itself at a distinct disadvantage in the field. They couldn't give chase, nor could they engage in mounted combat.

For this reason, in 1832, Congress authorized the creation of six companies of mounted volunteers for what was then termed "the defense of the frontier." Traditional handwringing over the expense occurred in Congress, but a budget was passed.

At that point in time, the American frontier was considered, in part, the Illinois Territory, comprising what would later become the states of Illinois, Wisconsin, the eastern portion of Minnesota, and the western portion of the upper peninsula of Michigan. Organized along the lines of militias, local men (or frontiersmen) were recruited. The enlistment period for the volunteer cavalry lasted one year at the meager pay rate of one dollar per day. The reporting volunteers supplied their own mounts and gear, meaning the quality of their horses and their riding abilities varied greatly. It seems probable that many may have left their best horses at home and out of harm's way.

By most accounts dating from that time, the army supplied very little in the way of materiel—leaving the volunteers cold, wet, hungry . . . and up to their own devices.

While that early experiment of using a mounted frontier defense only lasted one year, it convinced many of the benefit, and in fact the need, of having such a force readily available. Some type of patrol was needed to guard the government's interests and to protect the western settlers—wherever that western frontier or boundary might have been drawn in a given year. Borders or territories were fluid in those early times. And while the use of volunteers may have been born out of necessity, their services were not considered an overwhelming success by contemporaries. Secretary of War Lewis Cass reported to Congress on November 15, 1832, that the volunteers cost $279,530, while dragoons (viewed as a formal or professional class of mounted infantry who used horses but dismounted to fight) would have cost $143,580 in comparison. Beyond the monetary differential, the shortcomings of the volunteer "experiment" likely came down to the weakness of horses the volunteers rode and volunteer discipline, or lack thereof.[2] Reports of widespread drunkenness or impairment occurred, along with political maneuvering and self-interests on all sides.

Cass supported the idea of a mounted force to provide a measure of security and defense against hostiles, clearly preferring a formal force, rather than a ragtag assemblage of "expensive" and somewhat unreliable frontiersmen. On March 2, 1833, President Andrew Jackson signed a bill creating the First Regiment of US Dragoons, and the US government found itself back in the riding horse acquisition and supply business after having been on hiatus since the end of the War of 1812. This governmental equine supply and remount business would continue from that 1833 point forward until May of 1944.

Men started arriving at the Jefferson Barracks in Lemay, Missouri, during the summer of 1833—where they found that quarters and stables had not yet been built, nor had any of the requisitioned equipment arrived. By October 1833, conditions were improved, progress was made, and the necessary infrastructure was constructed. Enough horses arrived to mount three companies—the precise number of horses and men remain vague since companies varied in size. Regardless, many of the officers and the men were former members of the Battalion of Mounted Rangers who served in the Black Hawk War only one year earlier in 1832.

During the summer of 1834, the First Dragoons were sent to Fort Gibson in the Arkansas Territory (now Muskogee County, Oklahoma). The intent was to march across the plains in a type of discovery mission to visit the Kiowa, Comanches, and the Pawnee peoples. George Catlin, the noted artist, and other civilians, accompanied the five-hundred-man expedition, which started out under the auspices of General Henry Leavenworth. Although this expedition was considered a peaceful endeavor, as witnessed by the inclusion of civilians, no doubt it also served as a test of the utility of mounted troops on the vast American plains.

The First Dragoons had a remarkably bad time of it, and so did their mounts.

The expedition set off in the traditionally hot and humid month of July. On the way to Fort Gibson, no hostilities took place—except against nature. Under the blazing summer sun, the land the cavalry crossed was gripped by drought. Even worse, an unknown malady or disease took hold among both the men and their mounts.

On the very first day, some of the men were forced to turn back.

LETTER—No. 40.
MOUTH OF FALSE WASHITA

Since I wrote my last Letter from this place, I have been detained here with the rest of the cavalcade from the extraordinary sickness which is afflicting the regiment, and actually threatening to arrest its progress.

It was, as I wrote the other day, the expectation of the commanding officer that we should have been by this time recruited and recovered from sickness, and ready to start again on our march; but since I wrote nearly one half of the command, and included amongst them, several officers, with General Leavenworth, have been thrown upon their backs, with the prevailing epidemic, a slow and distressing bilious fever. The horses of the regiment are also sick, about an equal proportion, and seemingly suffering with the same disease. They are daily dying, and men are calling sick, and General Leavenworth has ordered Col. Dodge to select all the men, and all the horses that are able to proceed, and be off to-morrow at nine o'clock upon the march towards the Camanchees [sic], in hopes thereby to preserve the health of the men, and make the most rapid advance towards the extreme point of destination.[3]

This letter was written by the noted artist and civilian George Catlin.

General Leavenworth led the beginning stages of this expedition with the expectation of accompanying the party for two hundred miles. At that time, buffalo and wild game remained abundant in that area. The general fell from his horse while hunting buffalo, and as a result was left with other invalids near modern-day Kingston, Oklahoma, in an area called the Cross Timbers. The general unfortunately succumbed to either his injuries or sickness—accounts are unclear. He died on July 21, 1834, before he could be taken back to Fort Gibson.

Of the four hundred or so troops that began with the expedition, only 250 men were fit to continue by the time they had traveled two hundred miles. Colonel Dodge assumed command, and the remainder of the men proceeded across the plains in the withering heat, and if accounts are to be believed, only finding water in buffalo wallows. Eventually, they rested along the banks of the Canadian River, still sick and suffering—both men and mounts dying daily. George Catlin recorded that the regiment lost one-third of its officers, men, and mounts. But while the mounts broke and died, Catlin himself rode on a Comanche pony he believed thrived in the terrain and conditions.

This turns out to be an important point.

EARLY CAVALRY HORSES

Very few details are known about the quality or characteristics of the regiment's horses on Leavenworth's expedition. Purchasing officers of the time were provided with general guidelines: that the geldings (the horses had to be geldings) should stand between fifteen and sixteen hands high, be aged between four and nine years old, and their coats should be solid colors.

In 1845 another exploration of the western American plains set forth—this time under the leadership of Colonel Stephen W. Kearny. Marching along what would come to be known as the Oregon Trail (a route discovered in 1812 by Robert Stuart of the Pacific Fur Company[4]) with five companies of dragoons, the purpose of Kearny's mission was to impress the Plains Tribes with the might of the US Army. The march continued across what would become Nebraska up to South Pass, Wyoming. Kearny and the dragoons then turned south to continue on to Bent's Fort in what would later become the Colorado Territory. In ninety-nine days, this expedition traveled at least twenty-two hundred miles. While some sickness was reported and not all of the animals survived,

Kearny's march was not the disaster that Leavenworth's initial expedition proved.

When the Mexican–American War broke out in 1846, Congress authorized the formation of a third regiment of dragoons and volunteer cavalry commands. Locating and procuring enough horses to mount this new regiment proved to be a quartermaster's nightmare.

Some conception of the scope of quartermaster activities can be gleaned from the 1,556 wagons, 459 horses, 3,658 draft mules, 516 pack mules, and 14,904 oxen furnished to the Army of the West in the fiscal year 1846–1847 and the two thousand wagons and thousands of animals provided for the Chihuahua expedition.[5]

Contemporary claims were made that those horses were purchased without careful scrutiny, meaning that price was the overriding concern. According to reports at the time, few mounts were entirely saddle broken. Beyond that very basic qualification, officers swore that the supplied animals were nothing more than overage, worn-out plow horses with bad habits.[6]

The vast Western United States spread from the Mississippi River in the east to the setting sun over the Pacific Ocean in the west, to the frigid northern plains of Montana down to the border of Mexico. In reality, borders don't exist for horses. There are only miles and miles of endless terrain hosting the varied weather of the different seasons—cold northern blizzards, blistering sun in the deserts, and constant winds rushing over the badlands and across the plains.

Mention was made by the Americans and British who traveled past the great Mississippi River of the massive horse herds they encountered roaming wild in the western portion of the country. Lt. Ulysses S. Grant wrote while serving in the Mexican American War during 1846:

The country was a rolling prairie, and, from the higher ground, the vision was obstructed only by the earth's curvature. As far as the eye could reach to our right, the herd extended. To the left, it extended equally. There was no estimating the number of animals in it; I have no idea that they could all have been corralled in the State of Rhode Island, or Delaware, at one time. If they had been, they would have been so thick that the pasturage would have given out the first day. People who saw the Southern herd of buffalo, fifteen or twenty years ago, can appreciate the size of the Texas band of wild horses in 1846.[7]

An avid horseman himself, no doubt Grant was delighted by the sight of the wild horses. While serving in that war, Grant acted as the regimental quartermaster in the 4th US Infantry. That said, he still saw his fair share of combat.

Locked in fierce street by street fighting, Grant was forward with several companies when ammunition was nearly gone. He mounted a horse, kicked a leg over the saddle, and hung low on the horse's neck and flank, then raced the animal to the rear. Then after gaining help and ammunition, he returned under intense fire again, being fired at street by street, and amazingly arrived to resupply his regiment unharmed.[8]

Once the war ended in 1848, the US Army retained only three mounted divisions: The 1st Dragoons, the 2nd Dragoons, and the Regiment of Mounted Riflemen to protect the settlers moving westward.

In 1855, Congress realized that wasn't enough. They authorized the formation of two additional regiments: the 1st and 2nd Cavalry. In August of 1855, the 1st Cavalry was assigned to Leavenworth, Kansas, and the 2nd Cavalry established Fort Worth along the Trinity River in Texas. This expansion of mounted troops meant an increased need for horses. The math showed that most men required at least two mounts per year, especially if the mount and rider were involved in arduous duties. Horses, naturally, could become lost, stolen, killed, or incapacitated in one way or another. Muscle strains and lameness were a fact of life. Fresh remounts would prove critical in all operations and always remained a point of concern.

More rules and regulations were issued.

Cost per animal could not exceed $125 per head. Given current dollars, that would equate in today's dollars to $4,862 per mount. In the 1850s, in the attempt to procure better horses, the army experimented with the notion of setting up a "Board of Survey." The idea at the time held that horses would be purchased conditionally upon the review of such a board for the final purchase decision. The Board of Survey consisted of at least two officers who provided final approval prior to the animal's acceptance.

By most accounts, that "new" system worked fairly well.

In 1861, the three separate mounted groups were recognized as cavalry. The 1st Dragoons became the 1st Cavalry, and the other regiments were named the 2nd through the 6th according to the chronological dates they were activated. The 2nd Dragoons became the 6th Cavalry as a result of this chronological progression. As is obvious by the year, the American Civil War loomed close upon the horizon. On April 12, 1861, Fort Sumner came under fire, and the war commenced.

The Civil War falls beyond the scope of this book, except for the topic of horses. By the end of the war in 1865, the US Cavalry consisted of

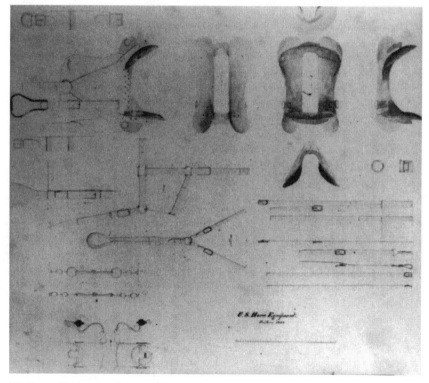

US Horse Equipment Pattern 1854. Note Saddle.
LIBRARY OF CONGRESS.

272 regiments, forty-five battalions, and seventy-eight companies. These numbers do not include the Confederate forces, who required that all cavalry men supply their own mounts. Viewing this through a Federal (Union) lens, as previously illustrated, the quartermasters experienced difficulties in supplying pre-war needs. During the Civil War, the cavalry men had to supply their own mounts and were compensated between forty and fifty cents per day for the usage of their horse(s). The quality of the equines varied greatly, as it had previously when riders supplied their own mounts. In 1862, all "public animal" procurement was transferred back to the quartermasters in an attempt to improve quality, quantity, and availability. The Quartermaster Corps created two different branches: one for field artillery (draft horses and mules) and the other for cavalry remounts.

> As far back as our Civil War . . . great difficulties were encountered in purchasing and caring for horses and mules and a woeful lack of knowledge of the care of animals in the hands of troops. At the outbreak of the Civil War two separate and distinct army agencies were charged with the procurement of animals, neither of which was properly organized, viz., The Quartermaster General's Office, which purchased draft horses and mules, and the Cavalry Bureau, which purchased Cavalry horses. It took two years to bring our army authorities at that time to a realization of the fact that animal affairs should be handled by an agency charged solely with that duty. A proper organization would, of course, have been one agency charged with the purchase of all animals for the Army. There was . . . much difficulty experienced . . . owing to the lack of care of animals and animal transportation. Special inspectors were appointed on the army staffs and they were given wide authority to correct these evils. However, affairs reached such a bad state that orders were issued authorizing the transfer of Cavalry officers, and even of whole Cavalry commands, to the Infantry, if found neglecting their animals.[9]

Once again, this is where another phenomenon raised its head: how to defraud a US government agency. The new Cavalry Remount Bureau encountered numerous problems: "Officers and quartermasters obtained 150,000 mounts during the initial phase of the war; the total amount spent for them was nearly $20,000,000. The announced average price paid, $133.33, was misleading. Either hundreds of horses cost over $400.00 each, or certain officers had defrauded the government."[10]

As the tide turned against the Confederacy, captured mounts became available, as did mounts for purchase at bargain prices. In Memphis, Tennessee, in 1862, a quartermaster purchased seven hundred saddle horses for $27,850, which equated to less than forty dollars per horse.[11]

On May 2, 1863, the Cavalry Bureau was created, largely in response to accusations of fraud and corruption. Although the Quartermaster Corp remained in charge, it was not allowed to purchase artillery or cavalry horses without the express order of the chief of the Cavalry Bureau. Six depots were created to receive horses and to rehabilitate mounts as needed. The depot for the western command was located near St. Louis, Missouri. This new governing body set more rigid standards for the care of the horses by requiring a monthly inspection and by grading companies in the field. Despite improvements, problems still existed, and leadership changed too frequently to prove truly effective. That changed in 1864 under the auspices of Maj. Gen. James Harrison Wilson. The new standards gained traction, and Wilson managed to stop the widespread graft. Under his leadership, horse dealers were arrested for passing off unhealthy horses or for bribing, or attempting to bribe, officers. While the quality of the mounts reportedly did not improve under his guidance, the Cavalry Bureau became a far more honest operation. Nevertheless, in 1866, it was disbanded.

This was also the year the US Army had to deal with their surplus of horses.

With the end of the Civil War, "too many horses remained" in prevailing estimations. A total of 104,000 horses were "condemned"—meaning no longer required. Just 3,829 "serviceable" mounts were retained for the cavalry. The vast majority were auctioned off, and many complaints came in from the recipients of the 3,829 retained mounts, who deemed their quality as inferior.

Whether the horses truly were inferior or were simply a topic for complaining is likely never to be known.

The responsibility for procuring horses remained with the quartermasters of the seven military districts, and the greatest amount paid for a horse remained at $125. One interesting point of note is that during these years, white hooves were considered inferior to dark hooves. (Structurally, there should be no difference since it is simply color pigmentation; however, there are people to this day who are convinced that white hoofs are slightly softer.) Horse dealers and sellers seldom tried to sell an animal to the army who had more than one white hoof—thereby excluding any number of perfectly serviceable animals due to the myth that was, at the time, believed to be a genuine structural flaw.

The military adhered, as best they could, to their guidelines.

The procured horses were expected to be from five to nine years old and weigh between 900 and 1,050 pounds. Most of the "art" of horse buying came in the assessment of composition. Powerful hindquarters with weak shoulders and chests, for example, made for an unbalanced horse. The army started measuring to determine whether, proportionally, a horse was considered "in balance." As previously, the requirements remained for the mount to stand between fifteen and sixteen hands high with clearly defined muscles. Withers were of particular importance. As anyone who has fit a saddle to a horse knows that the withers play a large part in how a saddle fits and holds. The army did its best to make certain that regulation army saddles would fit the horses comfortably and well.

Whenever it became necessary to purchase a mixed-blood horse (usually meaning a partial Mustang or Indian Pony), the height requirement dropped down to a minimum of fourteen and a half hands. As time progressed, the cavalry would become increasingly in favor of the mixed-blood horses.[12] As George Catlin noted back in 1834 with his thriving "Comanche pony," the western horses (meaning non-Thoroughbreds) performed well in western conditions.

Horse Induction into the Western Cavalry

Once inspected and passed fit for the cavalry, horses were branded with the initials *U.S.* on the left shoulder. They might have a tattoo on the left thigh representing the soldier's company and regiment.[13]

After the Civil War and during the Plains Indian War years, it is an unfortunate fact that many horses were lost due to battle, starvation, and hard marches. In 1875 and 1876 (remember that the Battle of the Little

Bighorn happened in 1876), the cavalry lost 1,376 mounts. Troops experimented with Texas cow ponies, but weighing in between 750 and 800 pounds, they were not up to the task of carrying 200 to 250 pounds day after day, which is the approximate weight of a soldier, saddle, guns, and provisions.

The difficulty in chasing skilled American Indians with infantry was widely recognized, but the mounted arm faced its own special problems:

> Hardworked [sic] cavalry mounts required grain, not just hay or grazing. Since full daily forage for one horse came to 14 pounds of hay, or 12 pounds of grain, this posed a supply problem of towering magnitude. Furnishing forage at isolated frontier posts was a never-ending headache and a heavy expense. Local contractors usually cut and delivered hay, but sometimes this chore fell to the troops, diverting them from military duties.
>
> These garrison problems exploded as soon as the cavalry took the field. Every extended campaign demanded slow and extensive wagon trains, and steamboats when possible, to transport mountains of forage, rations, ammunitions. . . . Depots then had to be guarded, preferably by infantry, since they consumed less stores themselves.[14]

Up to this point in the cavalry's history, the keen reader must have noted the lack of discussion concerning veterinary services. Plain and simple, there weren't any beyond what an observant farrier might provide. During the Civil War, this lack of expertise became apparent. In July 1866, Congress authorized four new cavalry units, which would be numbered the 7th through the 10th. Upon the recommendation of regimental officers, two veterinary surgeons were assigned to each new regiment. For some reason, the old regiments were still expected to muddle through without. Regardless, this assignment of veterinarians amounted to an advancement in the care of cavalry horses. The senior veterinarian would receive pay in the amount of one hundred dollars per month, and his junior would receive seventy-five dollars per month. That said, qualifications for these new positions were not specified until 1879, when the veterinarian posts were restricted to graduates of recognized veterinarian colleges.

Curiously, this inequity between the "new" and "old" units receiving veterinary care would remain in place for another thirty-three years, ending in 1899.[15]

THE 7TH CAVALRY

Custer's famed 7th Cavalry was one of the "new" regiments that received veterinary services. Dr. Stein arrived on April 17, 1876, as the senior veterinarian for the upcoming campaign of the Little Bighorn. Stein's first duty was to inspect the cavalry horses in preparation for the expedition and to recondition those not up to standard. Likewise, he also had to condemn horses truly unserviceable. According to the regimental returns, the 7th Cavalry began the month of April with a total of 722 horses, of which thirty-nine were unserviceable. According to the *Monthly Returns, 7th US Cavalry, 1876*, by the end of the month Dr. Stein had reduced the total number of mounts to 683, of which he pronounced ten as unserviceable. On May 8, Regimental Special Order No. 36 detailed Pvt. Martin Kefoyle of Company G to daily duty as his assistant as shown in *7th Cavalry Order Book, 1876*.[16]

A depiction of Indian battle and massacre near Fort Philip Kearney, Dakotah Territory, December 21, 1866.
LIBRARY OF CONGRESS.

Specific horses of the ill-fated campaign will be discussed in another chapter.

After Little Bighorn, in August 1876, Gen. George Crook attempted to track down Crazy Horse and other enemies, effectively bringing the battle to them. Once again, events did not proceed according to script. Unwilling to let the Sioux and others gather strength and prepare for battle on their own terms, General Crook set out in pursuit, leaving behind the supply wagons and relying upon mules to carry needed provisions and supplies. The men only carried what they wore and one blanket. Tents were not packed. This was a light cavalry moving at a hurried pace.

Despite the summer month, apparently it rained almost constantly, and grass and forage were hard to locate. By the time Crook and his men arrived where they expected to locate the tribes, they had already scattered. Worried that they might attack the Dakota mining camps such as Deadwood, Crook turned southward for another seven-day march with only two days of provisions. Men became ill, horses broke down, and some of those horses were eaten. The mounted cavalry ended up capturing a Sioux camp stocked with dried buffalo meat; their horse herds provided remounts for Crook's troops. On September 15, Crook and his men finally reached what is now called Crook City in the Black Hills. The general sent the following message to General Sheridan:

We had a very hard march from Heart River, for 80 consecutive miles we did not have a particle of wood, only a little dry grass which was insufficient even to cook coffee for the men. During the greater portion of the time we were drenched by cold rains which made travelling very heavy. A great many of the animals gave out and had to be abandoned, the others are now in such weak condition that the greater number of them will not be able to resume the campaign until after a reasonable rest. I should like to have about 500 horses, preferably the half-breed horses raised on the Laramie Plains or in the vicinity of Denver and acclimated to this country. I intend to carry out the programme mentioned in my last dispatch via Fort Laramie and shall remain in the vicinity of Deadwood until the arrival of my wagon train.

(signed) General Crook.[17]

This marks the point where the eastern thoroughbreds, although perhaps superior in appearance, were no longer so strongly preferred over the lowly western horse. Whether they were called Mustangs, half-breed, cow ponies, or California or Texas horses, there were some definite advantages in the native species. First, the larger eastern cavalry horses required a diet of hay and grain. Hearty and accustomed to the climate and terrain, native horses subsisted on grass and didn't lose weight because of it. They kept going day after day.

A preferred combination of the time was the offspring of a ranch mare and a blooded stallion, as these horses fared well on hard campaigns. In the 1870s and 1880s during the Apache campaigns throughout New Mexico, Arizona, and Mexico, the 9th Cavalry rode to Fort Bayard, New Mexico, on Missouri horses. After four months of campaigning, these horses were found unfit for service.

In 1876, the 6th Cavalry was sent to New Mexico to relieve the 9th Cavalry. Accounts record that the two divisions exchanged horses. Reportedly, the 6th Cavalry felt very displeased with the trade when they handed over their eastern mounts. Opinions were voiced. However, after four months of hard riding, the 6th Cavalry did not lose a single mount of the western-bred horses.

That fortunate fact came before the pursuit of Victorio in the rugged New Mexican desert terrain. Due to the lack of water and the severe and arid landscape, many of even the western-bred horses did not survive that demanding round of hardships. Many perished as a result of wounds and hardship.

HORSE HANDLING ABILITIES AND CARE

Strange but true: Not all the cavalry soldiers actually proved to be good, or even adequate, riders, at least in the beginning of their commissions.

One might think the ability to ride well would have been a prerequisite, but that appears not to be the case. This lack of horsemanship or ability might also account for some of the prejudice against the so-called Mustangs and the cow and Indian ponies. Many members of the cavalry considered the western "native" horse too small, too vicious, and ill-formed. If the horse could be saddle-broken and trained not to bite or kick, it proved its worth in its ability to cover large distances (such as forty miles) day after day. In 1883, the cavalry was allowed to purchase mounts directly from ranchers, farmers, and even tribes. This ability to "direct source" made it easier to purchase durable range horses from western locations. Free from disease and often quick learners, these horses proved high-spirited and somewhat difficult for poor riders to handle. Also, as all riders know, horses size up their riders as much as the rider sizes up the horse.

The favorite deflection of poor horsemen was to aim the blame at the quartermasters for procuring poor mounts.

This was not necessarily so, claimed Brig. Gen. O. O. Howard, known to his troops as "Old Prayer Book." After the Nez Perce War, or Chief Joseph's War, he wrote a report denouncing the cavalrymen's lack of ability. Perhaps the experiences stem from June 22, 1877, when 255 of his men spent the next two and a half weeks chasing over rough terrain and crossing difficult, and flooded, rivers.[18] One officer wrote, "The height of the men's ambitions seemed to be to be able to stick to their horse's back from one camp to another. . . . In fact, I never saw so many indifferent horsemen before."[19]

Brigadier General Howard would also later comment on the men's lack of horse handling or riding abilities, stating that entire companies could not make their horses swim across the Salmon River and had to be ferried over "two and four at a time."[20] At the Clearwater River, the same scene replayed itself. "Few indeed, if any, of our soldiers could be made to swim their horses mounted . . . the coaxing, driving, pounding, striking, shouting, chasing, plunging into water, and emerging on the same side all along for half a mile . . . will not soon be forgotten by those of us who witnessed the exhibition."[21]

The fact of the matter remained that each troop commander was responsible for training his own men. If an officer was not a proficient horseman, he wouldn't be able to train his troops well. Apparently, a fair percentage of officers sent from West Point did not know much about horses. One discouraged officer claimed that he would welcome company officers who were just good riders. "By knowing how to ride," he emphasized, "I do not mean the possession of what is termed a military seat, but the ability to manage average horses, and the feeling that he and his horse are one, and not distinct and uncongenial spirits."[22]

None of this meant that the riders didn't care about their mounts. While anecdotal evidence is sparce:

> About noon the "strikers," who carried the haversacks, were called, and the different messes had their luncheon . . . when the haversacks were opened, the horses usually stopped grazing and put their noses near their riders faces and asked very plainly to share the hardtack: if their polite request did not receive attention they would paw the ground, or even strike their riders. The old soldier was generally willing to share with his beast.[23]

That paints quite a picture.

Western Horse Trivia

The 1st Cavalry Division has an Official Horse Detachment. The 1st Cavalry is known for its equestrian heritage. Although that skill is no longer used in battle, they have kept their Horse Cavalry Detachment alive and trotting. Today, the Horse Cavalry Detachment is used for ceremonial and recruitment purposes and preserves the division's horseback riding roots.[24]

NOTES

1. Online Etymology Dictionary, "Cavalry," https://www.etymonline.com/word/cavalry#etymonline_v_8303.

2. Willis B. Hughes, "The First Dragoons on the Western Frontier 1834–1846," *Arizona and the West* 12, 2 (1970): 117.

3. George Catlin, *Letters and Notes on the Manners, Customs and Conditions of the North American Indians: Written During Eight Years of Travels Among the Wildest Tribes of Indians in North America*, London, England: Tilt and Bogue Fleet Street, 1842.

4. William Lang, "Essay: Oregon Trail," https://www.oregonencyclopedia.org/articles/oregon_trail/#:~:text=The%20Oregon%20Trail%20developed%20from,man%20returning%20from%20Fort%20Astor.

5. Alvin P. Stauffer, "Supply of the First American Overseas Expeditionary Force: The Quartermaster's Department and the Mexican War," *Quartermaster Review*, May–June 1950, http://old.quartermasterfoundation.org/quartermaster_department_mexican_war.htm.

6. Emmett M. Essen, III, *Western Horse Tales*, edited by Don Worcester, Plano, TX: Republic of Texas Press, 1994, 242.

7. Ulysses S. Grant, *The Personal Memoirs of Ulysses S. Grant*, https://www-tc.pbs.org/wgbh/americanexperience/media/filer_public/00/9d/009d03b6-2f0c-4197-a13d-219044df1182/grant_memoirs.pdf.

8. Sherman Fleek, "Grant in Mexico: One of the Most Unjust (Wars) Ever Waged," January 31, 2019.

9. A. A. Cedarwald, *The Quartermaster Review—November–December 1928*. https://www.quartermasterfoundation.org/the-remount-service-past-and-present.

10. Essen, *Western Horse Tales*, 245.

11. Essen, *Western Horse Tales*, 245.

12. Essen, *Western Horse Tales*, 246–47.

13. Jeremy Agnew, *Life of a Soldier on the Western Frontier*, Missoula, MT: Mountain Press Publishing Company, 2008, 184.

14. John S. Gray, "Veterinary Service on Custer's Last Campaign," *Kansas Historical Society* 3, 3 (Autumn 1977), https://www.kshs.org/p/veterinary-service-on-custer-s-last-campaign/13275#Note2.

15. Gray, "Veterinary Service."

16. Gray, "Veterinary Service."

17. "Oral History of the Dakotah Tribes 1800s–1945 as Told to Colonel A. B. Welch First White Man Adopted By the Sioux Nation," https://www.welchdakotapapers.com/2011/11/little-big-horn-general-shermans-command-watching-for-and-searching-for-sitting-bull-january-thru-october-1876/#film-0585.

18. Essen, *Western Horse Tales*, 257; John A. Carpenter, "General Howard and the Nez Perce War of 1877," *The Pacific Northwest Quarterly* 49, 4 (1958): 134.

19. Essen, *Western Horse Tales*, 257.

20. Essen, *Western Horse Tales*, 257.

21. Essen, *Western Horse Tales*, 257.

22. Essen, *Western Horse Tales*, 258.

23. Elizabeth Atwood Lawrence, *His Very Silence Speaks: Comanche—the Horse Who Survived Custer's Last Stand*, Detroit, MI: Wayne State University Press, 1989, 58.

24. United Service Organizations, "9 Must-Know Facts about the Army's 1st Cavalry Division," https://www.uso.org/stories/2465-9-must-know-facts-about-the-army-s-1st-cavalry-division-for-its-birthday#:~:text=9%20Must-Know%20Facts%20about%20the%20Army%27s%201st%20Cavalry,to%20Make%20it%20Into%20Manila.%20...%20More%20items.

CHAPTER 4

THE LEAVENWORTH AND PIKE'S PEAK EXPRESS COMPANY [AKA THE PONY EXPRESS]— A LEGEND IN ITS OWN TIME, 1860–1861

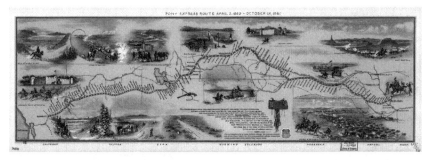

Pony Express Route, April 3, 1861–October 24, 1861. Jackson, Driggs, and the Union Pacific Railroad Company.
LIBRARY OF CONGRESS.

NEVER HAS ONE SINGLE ENDEAVOR SO CAPTURED THE IMAGINATION OF the nation. And never have facts been so up for grabs concerning such a momentous event. Or at least it certainly feels that way. As a historical, recorded, and documented business, the Pony Express remains frustratingly elusive and unknowable. In hindsight, 160 years later, the modern enthusiast quests for a depth of knowledge and details concerning the events. "The Pony's" contemporaries, founders, and employees could never have considered their experiences lasting the test of time. As a result, the Pony Express instead sparked a later-day reckoning—an opportunity for the details and "facts" to be presented with the benefit of hindsight, with plenty of embellishment filled in afterwards. Many men came forward as self-proclaimed participants, seeking aggrandizement, once they realized how powerfully the enterprise had captured the popular imagination.

Any association, no matter how fleeting, with the doomed enterprise remained difficult to prove. Tenuous claims nevertheless guaranteed a measure of fame that could translate into money, notoriety, or free drinks in exchange for tales of wild rides that may, or may not, have taken place.

Steeped in mystery and lore, the Pony Express Oath of Office is a fine place to start with this uniquely American undertaking:

> I _____, do hereby swear, before the great and Living God, that during my engagement, and while I am in the employ of Russell, Majors & Waddell, I will, under no circumstances, use profane language; that I will drink no intoxicating liquors; that I will not quarrel or fight with any other employee of the firm, and that in every respect I will conduct myself honestly, be faithful to my duties, and so direct all my acts as to win the confidence of my employers. So help me God.[1]

To modern readers, and likely to even some of the applicants swearing the oath—right hand on the Bible and the left held high—the requirements contained within must have seemed like a tall order indeed. Especially the promise to forgo profane language and liquor—two frontier staples. The Pony Express Oath of Office illuminates the character of the employers more so than of the applicants—and one of the founders in particular. The deeply religious Alexander Majors undoubtedly provided the driving force behind the administration of the oath.

He also handed out small leatherbound Bibles to his riders. Which, considering weight limitations, strikes as a bit surprising. Obviously, Majors thought the moral investment well worth making.

But back to the oath. That surprising content indeed formed the basis of the rider's employment with the fabled Pony Express. That, and they had to be able to handle a horse and to ride. Ride very fast.

In the days before the telegraph, the Pony Express was a short-lived service that has seared itself into the collective American imagination. Only in operation from the years 1860 to 1861, the Pony Express sought to fulfill an audacious mission: to deliver the mail across the vast American West. From April 3, 1860, through October 24, 1861, the route ran from St. Joseph, Missouri, to Sacramento, California. The thrill of the Pony Express sprang largely from its daring speed. "The Pony" riders covered a vast, barren, and hostile distance of over eighteen hundred miles in ten days. *Ten days.*

It was a logistical marvel, and a logistical nightmare.

The Pony Express embodied the epitome of American *can-do-edness*, and it served a very real need. The problem with legends and innovation is that often that gloriousness didn't come cheap. The hard truth of the matter of their services provided and sold was that many people did not care to spend the five dollars to send a letter—the equivalent of $183.21 in today's dollars. Nevertheless, the legend sprang to life and took hold of popular imagination like nothing else during its time.

That legend lost a staggering two hundred thousand dollars by the time it ceased operations a short eighteen months later. That loss equates to $7,328,400 in current dollars.

The firm of Russell, Majors and Waddell needed 153 stations, somewhere between four hundred to five hundred good horses, and about eighty dependable riders. Those fundamental requirements were just the bare minimum of the infrastructure needed for the operations. Due to the staggering investment required in the undertaking, the private firm needed government postal contracts to survive, much less turn a profit.

While earmarked lucrative government contracts never held much allure, the actual Pony Express and its riders were truly the talk of the country.

The westbound inauguration of the Pony Express on April 3, 1860, feted by a grand affair in St. Joseph, Missouri, started out characteristically enigmatic for an enigmatic enterprise. The riders presumably were toasted and admired the night before the momentous send off at the lavish Patee House's ballroom, but there is no proof. Surely a crowd gathered the following day to see the rider off at the predetermined 4:00 p.m., but events transpired against that expected departure time. The US post, expected to arrive by rail, was delayed by two and a half hours. The train failed to leave Detroit on time. By all accounts, the train engineers did their utmost to make up that lost time. Passengers on board recorded the fearsome speed as the train hurtled, albeit late, toward their date with history.

The waiting rider, whose name remarkably defies verification as well (although he is often assumed to be Johnnie Fry, there is some claim that the rider's identity might have been that of Billy Richardson[2]) failed to leave St. Joseph until 7:15 that night when the train-bound post finally arrived.

The eastbound mail, carried by either Harry Roff or James Randall,[3] left Sacramento at noon with no known delays at their start.

Remarkably, the riders and the men who awaited their turn on the cross-country relay managed to make up the lost time on that first run, and the mail was delivered within the promised ten days. That delayed westbound delivery crossed the wide country and arrived in Sacramento on April 14, 1860, slightly after midnight. The eastbound delivery crossed the same desolate country to reach St. Joseph at 5:00 p.m.

The careful reader will notice the uncertainty as to the *exact* identity of those first Pony Express riders. That's the thing about the Pony Express. There's a whole lot of supposed facts and information (or lack thereof) up for debate and conjecture. Part of its appeal remains its mystery—and where the Pony Express is concerned, there is plenty of mystery to go around.

Next to nothing concerning the operation is 100 percent certain.

What is for certain was the physics that lightness equated to speed. The riders were likely small and wiry, reportedly special lightweight saddles were built (but once again, none survive), and the mail itself, written on thin paper, was protected by a carrier pouch called a mochila. Each rider covered about seventy-five to one hundred miles per shift and changed horses five to eight times during that time.

Reportedly only two minutes were allocated per change of mounts at each horse exchange.

The logistics of assembling the riders, the mounts, the stations, and the equipment required an enormous amount of planning. Beyond those basic assemblages came the timing and the layouts. The correct riders and stock had to be available for the runs and transfers at the right place, and at the correct time, for the relay to run without a hitch.

Beginning with the physical stations themselves, at least 190 locations are believed to have existed, but again, the details belonging to many of those have been lost to time. What is known is that there were two types of stations: "home" and "swing" stations. The Pony Express stations were planned out and usually spaced about five to twenty miles apart, dependent upon the location and the type and difficulty of the terrain.[4] Utilizing existing stagecoach stations, those outposts did double duty and serviced the Pony Express as well as the slower passenger stages. What is important to keep in mind is just how unsettled the vast stretches of territory were in the American West. The cavalry, emigrants, stagecoach lines, outlaws, and the Pony Express would all use whatever scarce infrastructure was available.

Not to mention, many of the stations were wildly remote and provided the only structure or assistance available for miles around.

New stations were built for the Pony Express as needed beyond what already existed, such as operations known as ranches. The Express' structures were built for purpose and not necessarily for longevity. Since they were located along commonly used trails, those stations were still located in the middle of next to nowhere. Constructed out of the local materials on hand, such as sod, adobe, log construction, dug outs, or any combination thereof, few beyond those constructed on either the eastern- or the western-most points on the route would have been constructed of brick or stone. The ranches used were often little more than watering holes, but those business enterprises provided a smattering of conveniences for travelers, such as places to sleep with meals served of varying qualities. Some of those home-distilled "ranche" whiskies went down in history as legendary rotgut. One account referred to it as "needle-gun whiskey, guaranteed to kill a mile away."[5]

"Swing," or relay, stations were simply places where riders switched their horses and continued along their designated route. Once again, numbers must be assumed, but it is thought that twenty-five home stations dotted along the route at intervals of sixty-five to one hundred miles apart.

At the stations, either "home" or "swing," the employees of the stage company were required to take care of the ponies and have them in readiness at the proper moment. The home stations had more substance and would have a station keeper or an agent in charge, and five or six "boys" to help with the chores and tasks in addition to the riders themselves.

Relay stations had just the one person in charge of caring for the horses.[6]

Backing up a bit on the configuration of the operations, the Pony Express route was split into five operating divisions, which impacts the discussion about the horses used. The eastern division came first and ran

The Persuit [sic], 1860, from J. H. Bufford's lithograph in Boston. Idealized setting of the Pony Express and the West capturing the element of dime-novel danger. Notice the expression in the horse's eye.
LIBRARY OF CONGRESS.

from St. Joseph to Fort Kearney, Nebraska (then in the Kansas Territory). The second division ran from Fort Kearney to Horseshoe, Wyoming (above Fort Laramie); the third division covered the distance between Horseshoe and Salt Lake City; the fourth division encompassed the route between Salt Lake and Roberts Creek, Nevada; and the fifth and final division was the segment between Roberts Creek and Sacramento.[7]

From the *Leavenworth Daily Times*, February 10, 1860:

WANTED

TWO HUNDRED GREY MARES, from four to seven years old, not to exceed fifteen hands high, well broke to the saddle, and Warranted Sound,

With black hoofs, and suitable for running the "Overland Poney [sic] Express."

JONES, RUSSELL & COMPANY[8]

And this on February 22, 1860:

The Pike's Peak Express left yesterday morning for Denver. There were two passengers, and a very large freight list. Among the articles, we noticed a lot of saddles and other riggings for the Pony Express. Mr. Van Vleit was the Messenger.[9]

The types of horses acquired for use by the Pony Express were, understandably, dependent upon available horses in the region where the divisions were located. Horses, no matter the breed or stock, had to be good. They had to have stamina and be able to outrun raiders and warriors, and had to be able to perform time and time again. On the eastern portion of the operations, "much blooded American stock"[10] seems to have been chosen. That many of these animals came from the US Army is indicated by the following item from the *Missouri Free Democrat*: "The stables of the Pony Express Company are being rapidly filled with horses bought from Captain McKissack at Leavenworth."[11] This raises a question as to why the US Army sold *good* horses to civilian contractors, but that answer may never be known for certain. True, there was a Fort Leavenworth located upon the banks of the Missouri River and established during 1827 to protect the travelers along the Santa Fe Trail. Perhaps they operated with a surplus, but it is doubtful whether their stock would have been considered of a high enough quality for the demands presented by the Pony Express.

Coming in the category of recollections after the fact, these opinions on the quality of the Pony Express horses have passed into history as truth. In a 1908 account, one Captain Levi Hensel of Pueblo, Colorado, is recorded as providing a letter stating:

> I had the contract to shoe the Overland Stage and Pony Express horses that ran from Kennekuk to Big Sandy up to the time I threw down my hammer and went into the army . . . sometimes they ran ponies in from Fort Kearney and beyond to be shod. The animals Johnnie Fry and Jim Beatley used to ride were the worst imps of Satan in the business. The only way I could master them was to throw them, get a rope around each foot, and to stake them out, and to have a man at the head and another at the body while I trimmed the hooves and nailed on the shoes. They would squeal and bite all the time I was working with them. It generally took half a day to shoe one of them. But travel! They never seemed to get tired.[12]

And another opinion: "We used to say that the company had bought up every mean, bucking, kicking horse that could be found."[13] It stands to reason that the horses were high-spirited, but it seems unlikely that they weren't rideable, as this man's descriptions would lead a reader to believe.

As any rider knows (but it bears repeating), these rides were not made at a flat-out gallop unless something was specifically wrong. True, the stereotypical image the Pony Express presents is of galloping riders crossing the wide-open empty. That type of speed was held in reserve for getting out of dangerous situations. Horses simply cannot last long distances at a gallop, especially over rough terrain. The routes and rides between stations were made at a good trot or easy canter, covering about ten to fifteen miles in an hour.

The western portion of the route utilized "pure Californian stock" and "half-breed" horses that proved unequalled for the rough western terrain. Other sources claim that the stock came of "mustangs, Morgans, pintos, and thoroughbreds."[14]

The largest stations had the most horses available. Guittard's Station in Kansas had a barn that could hold twenty-four horses. Cottonwood, also known as the Hollenberg Station, was the largest operation in Kansas boasting a barn that could hold one hundred horses. Faust's Station, also called East Rush Valley Station, located in Utah was also used to raise horses for the Express.[15] The riders were outfitted with company tack. The saddles used were likely little more than a tree, rigging, and a seat in the fashion of the McClellan saddle. McClellan saddles, invented in the mid-1850s, were used by the cavalry starting in 1859. Their conformation consisted of a hollowed out opening for the horse's spine to move unhindered. Fashioned for the comfort of the horse over that of the rider, there are people who use McClellan saddles and claim that they are not *un*comfortable. Some even like them today.

But back to the Pony Express. Once again, there is no known surviving saddle that was proven to be used by the Pony Express operations to examine. There are only suppositions on this theory.

The mochila carried the mail organized in four pouches—two in front of the stirrups and two behind—and had a hole cut for the saddle horn (if they had one) and the back of the cantle. The mochilas, designed for easy removal, could quickly be changed and placed on a fresh horse as the ride continued onward.

"WANTED. Young, skinny, wiry fellows. Not over 18. Must be expert riders. Willing to risk death daily. Orphans preferred." While the striking advertisement has claimed its place in lore, no proof has ever been found of its contemporaneous usage during the years 1860 and 1861. But it sure makes a good story, even if it came as an afterthought, or a notion with a notable amount of poetic license thrown in for good measure.

The riders, orphans or not, were paid good wages for the time. Again, recollections differ, and verification is impossible. Some riders recollected earning forty dollars per month, others one hundred dollars. The average

The overland Pony Express from a painting by George M. Ottinger.
LIBRARY OF CONGRESS.

is claimed to amount to fifty dollars, plus food and board at the stations. One rider named Elijah Nicholas Wilson recounted that riders were charged for their saddles (assuming the lightweight Pony design) and revolvers if they didn't already own a gun. Those costs were reportedly deducted from their wages.[16]

Danger was a rider's constant companion, as anyone who rides a horse on the trail can testify. The first tragedy happened fifteen days after the inaugural ride, when a rider leaving San Francisco traveling toward the east was killed. Traveling at speed at night, he didn't see an ox lying in the road . . . and obviously, neither did the horse. The rider was thrown, and his horse fell upon him, crushing him beneath. The rider died a short time later. Once again, however, no details such as the young man's name or location are provided in this account—just the fact that it "happened." There is historical documentation that four Pony Express riders were killed in fights with American Indians, one hanged for murder after he got drunk and killed a man (expressly against the Pony Oath), one man was killed in an unrelated accident (presumably the one crushed by his horse), and two froze to death.[17]

Alexander Majors, one of the partners of the Express, wrote an account of his life. In it was one chapter devoted to the Pony Express and its riders. Majors wrote:

> In the spring of 1860 Bolivar Roberts, superintendent of the Western Division of the Pony Express, came to Carson City, Nev., which was then in St. Mary's County, Utah, to engage riders and station men for a pony express route about to be established across the great plains by Russell, Majors & Waddell. In a few days fifty or sixty men were engaged, and started out across the Great American Desert to establish stations, etc. Among that number the writer can recall to memory the following: Bob Haslam ("Pony Bob"), Jay G. Kelley, Sam Gilson, Jim Gilson, Jim McNaughton, Bill McNaughton, Jose Zowgaltz, Mike Kelley, Jimmy Buckton, and "Irish Tom." At present "Pony Bob" is living on "the fat of the land" in Chicago. Sam and Jim Gilson are mining in Utah, and all the old "Pony" boys will rejoice to know they are now millionaires. The new mineral, gilsonite, was discovered by Sam Gilson. Mike Kelley is mining in Austin, Nev.; Jimmy Bucklin, "Black Sam," and the McNaughton boys are dead. William Carr was hanged in Carson City, for the murder of Bernard Cherry, his unfortunate death being the culmination of a quarrel begun months before, at Smith Creek Station. His was the first legal hanging in the Territory, the sentence being passed by Judge Cradlebaugh.[18]

At least the identity of the man hung for murder was explicitly identified.

The two men killed at the Williams Station on May 7, 1860, in an incident of violence that sparked the Pyramid Lake Indian War in Nevada and led to one of the greatest rides of US history.

Not that much (unsurprisingly) is known about the three Williams brothers named James, Oscar, and David, other than that they originally hailed from Maine. They were the proprietors of the Williams Station. A man named James O. Sullivan was designated as that station's keeper. Located approximately ten miles east of Buckland's Station, east of the Big Bend of the Carson River in Nevada, there's even a debate as to whether the Williams Station was utilized by the Pony Express. To add to the confusion, there are some references to this location as the Williams Ranch at Millers Station.

Whatever the case and the nature of the ranch, which could mean almost anything in those days, James O. Williams had been away from his station, and when he returned, he found his brothers Daniel and Oscar both dead. Again, it is unclear how many bodies may have been in the burnt-out building—perhaps three, other accounts say five. It seems likely that Sullivan, the station master, would have been one of the deceased. The stock and horses were stolen or driven off.

And more about the heroic ride later.

The best-known Pony riders are Robert "Pony Bob" Haslem and Johnny Fry.

Robert Haslam rode into history on account of an offer of a fifty-dollar bonus. Born in London, England, in 1840, he was part of the great Mormon migration into Utah. Bob was hired to help build some of the stations as the service was being set up and built—and when the mail began running, Haslam was assigned to Friday's Station near Lake Tahoe. His standard route ran from Friday's to Fort Churchill near present-day Silver Springs, Nevada. In May of 1860, Pony Bob started out from Friday's on what seemed a regular run. At Carson City, he rode up to the station, expecting to change horses. None was there, the rested mount having been requisitioned by the state militia to chase American Indians. Bob rode on to Buckland's station. There, his relief rider Johnson Richardson announced that with American Indians ready to fight, he wasn't risking his life for the US mail.

The station manager at that stop, W. C. Marley, offered Pony Bob fifty bucks if he kept on riding.

He took the money.

And he rode.

Riding to Cold Springs and then to Smith's Creek, poor Bob traveled nearly 140 miles from his initial station, perhaps even twenty or thirty more beyond even that estimate.

When Pony Bob reached Smith's station, he slept for a few hours, then awoke to take the mochila from the westbound rider. Retracing the route, he reached Cold Springs, where he found that American Indians had retaliated the day before. The station keeper lay dead, the buildings burned, and the horses driven off or, more likely, stolen.

He kept on riding.

When he finally reached the Sand Springs Station, he told the station keeper what he'd found. The keeper decided to abandon his post for safety and rode along with Bob. Both men made it to Carson Sink on May 13, 1860. There they found the station house barricaded by fifteen men, understandably preparing for and worried about a fight with the American Indians. According to the story, Bob Haslem continued on alone to Buckland's, where he began his regular run, back through Carson City and on to Friday's Station.

Pony Bob managed to deliver the mail through the most dangerous part of the route at the beginning of the Paiute Indian War, also known as the Pyramid Lake War.[19]

Johnny Fry, wiry and reportedly weighing less than 120 pounds soaking wet, built a similar reputation as a strong, talented rider. He may have been the first westbound rider. Then again, he may not have been. He rode for the Pony Express until May 1861. He would then join the Union army and serve in the Civil War. It is said that he died in 1863 at the hands of Quantrill's raiders in the Battle of Baxter Springs.

The telegraph ushered in a new age, and the final connection between east and west was made at Salt Lake City on October 24, 1861. The Pony Express ended, per contract, on October 26, 1861.

Buffalo Bill Cody was quick to capture the nostalgia associated with the Pony Express, featuring it in his Wild West shows of the 1890s, bolstering the Pony's reputation and helping to claim a corner of the American imagination.

Perhaps this often-quoted summary says it the best:

Through approximately eighteen months of variable weather, Indian disturbances, and almost insurmountable difficulties, the Express had faithfully discharged its responsibilities in such a manner as to win unstinted, unanimous praise. During that time 308 runs were made, covering a distance of 616,000 miles. On those runs, 34,753 letters were carried, with the loss of only one mochila. Of the total, 23,356 letters originated in California and 11,397 in the East. Estimated receipts were $91,404, of which the West supplied about two-thirds, or $60,844.[20]

Western Horse Trivia

The Pony Express required up to four hundred horses, as the riders swapped out their steeds up to ten times a ride.[21]

NOTES

1. National Postal Museum, "The Oath of Office," https://postalmuseum.si.edu/exhibition/remember-the-pony/the-oath-of-office.

2. National Park Service, "Frequently Asked Questions," https://www.nps.gov/poex/faqs.htm.

3. National Park Service, "Frequently Asked Questions."

4. National Pony Express Association, "Stations," https://nationalponyexpress.org/historic-pony-express-trail/stations/#:~:text=The%20Pony%20Express%20Used%20Over,used%20for%20"The%20Pony."

5. Nell Brown Propst, *The South Platte Trail: The Story of Colorado's Forgotten People*, Boulder, CO: Pruett Publishing, 1989, 30.

6. National Park Service, "Frequently Asked Questions."

7. National Park Service, "Organization and Operation of the Pony Express, 1860–1861," https://www.nps.gov/parkhistory/online_books/poex/hrs/hrs3a.htm#:~:text=The%20first%20division%20ran%20from,from%20Roberts%20Creek%20to%20Sacramento.

8. Kansas State Historical Society, https://www.kshs.org/publicat/khq/1959/1959winter_pony_express.pdf.

9. Kansas State Historical Society, https://www.kshs.org/publicat/khq/1959/1959winter_pony_express.pdf.

10. National Park Service, "Organization and Operation of the Pony Express, 1860–1861."

11. *Western Horseman*, "The Horses of the Pony Express," January–February 1942, https://westernhorseman.com/culture/out-west/the-horses-of-the-pony-express.

12. William Lightfoot Visscher, *A Thrilling and Truthful History of the Pony Express; or, Blazing the Westward Way, and Other Sketches and Incidents of Those Stirring Times*, Chicago, Rand McNally, 1908, 36.

13. Arthur Chapman, *The Pony Express; The Record of a Romantic Adventure in Business*, New York, NY: Cooper Square Publications, 1971, 288.

14. *Western Horseman*, "The Horses of the Pony Express."

15. Jim DeFelice, *West Like Lightning: The Brief, Legendary Ride of the Pony Express*, New York, NY: William Morrow, 2018, appendix.

16. DeFelice, *West Like Lightning*, 34–35.

17. National Park Service, "Frequently Asked Questions."

18. Alexander Majors, *Seventy Years on the Frontier*, Chicago, IL: Rand, McNally and Company Publishers, 1893, 187.

19. DeFelice, *West Like Lightning*, 184–85.

20. Raymond W. Settle, "The Pony Express—Heroic Effort, Tragic End," *Utah Historical Quarterly* 27, 2 (1959): 121–23.

21. Shaunacy Farro, "11 Facts about the Pony Express," *Mental Floss*, April 2, 2021, https://www.mentalfloss.com/article/537885/facts-about-pony-express.

CHAPTER 5

WESTERN SETTLEMENT

GIVEN THE IMPORTANCE OF THE HORSE ON THE SETTLEMENT OF THE West, it stands to reason that reliance upon the equines spawned related industries providing for their needs. As the Spaniards set up horse breeding *rancherias* during the reintroduction of the equine in North America, so did the western settlers in the mid- to late nineteenth century. While history books mention equines in passing, not enough emphasis is placed on the horses themselves, and the people who raised, trained, and handled the animals. In their own way, horses were very much a part of the emerging economy.

VAQUEROS AND CHARROS—EARLY HORSE HANDLERS

Thinking upon the Mexican cowboys known to history as vaqueros, a very distinctive image comes to mind. Whether it (undoubtedly) was enhanced by Hollywood, the term conjures a riot of colors, flashing conchos, decorated sombreros, colorful sarapes, and *chaperras* (chaps) or trousers with embroidery trailing down the sides like mariachi's charro outfits. No doubt, these colorful and thrilling outfits are partially later inventions, and the origins of their traditional finery were probably reserved for special occasions, but their outfits remain distinctive and striking.

In the vaqueros' or charros work-a-day world, more than likely, they dressed in a manner similar to the "American" cowboys. Working with horses is not the place to wear fancy clothing, as almost certainly, it will get ruined or, at the very least, dirty.

The term *charro*, in Mexico, historically refers to a horseman from the countryside, who worked on the haciendas and rural areas (rancheros). It was assumed that he performed all, or most, of his tasks on horseback, working as a vaquero, or cowboy. These men as a group became renowned for their superb horsemanship, skill in handling the lasso, and for their unique and fancy dress (when not actually performing such tasks as herding cattle, breaking horses, fixing fences, and the like).

The most notable example of "*charrería*" is General Emiliano Zapata, who was known before the Mexican Revolution as a skilled rider and horse tamer.

The term *vaqueros* comes from *vaca* or cow. Often in the Spanish language, the letter "v" is pronounced like a "b," hence the anglicized slang term for cowboys or "buckaroos" was derived from the Spanish. The Spanish were riding horses in the American Southwest and were the precursors to the "cowboys." The earliest horses for the Spaniards in the New World were of Spanish, Barb, and Arabian ancestry. A number of uniquely American (North and South) horse breeds were developed over time. Interestingly, a Spanish army Captain named Bernardo Vargas Machuca wrote in 1599 that he found "Mexican" horses to be the best and the finest.

> Horses, which were the most noble animal and of most use . . . so much so that there is no Spaniard who is unable to breed them and even the Indians, generally in the settled lands. And there is a large quantity of wild horses between Tucuman and the River Plate, but not so many as on the Windward Islands, for there are many there. The animal is used more for service than they are here [in Spain], for pack trains primarily use horses. . . . There are excellent parade horses and the stables are well established. The finest are Mexican but in general they are all good, for apart from being light and marvelously fast, they rein well and respond. . . . They have but one fault, that they are not high-steppers, and running well comes from this; but as they are low-steppers they charge better and are lighter, and a horse is not old at fourteen years.[1]

Those horses, or their offspring, likely roamed northward, some after escaping into the wild.

The vaqueros mastered other unique skills in their vocation. By most accounts, they were the inventors of the lasso and of its usage to control livestock. Derived from the Spanish word *lazo* (rope), the term *lasso* was coined in the early nineteenth century. Originally made with twisted leather hide and horsehair, the lasso "was what really separated [the vaqueros] from the rest of the horsemen that we'd seen,"[2] says Pablo A. Rangel, an independent historian who has studied the vaquero extensively.

Skillfully handling a lasso allowed vaqueros to contain wayward cattle:

> Horses, which were the most noble animal and of most use, God wished to greatly multiply, so much so that there is no Spaniard who is unable to breed them and even the Indians do so in the settled lands. . . . There are excellent parade horses, and the stables are well stocked. The finest are Mexican horses, but in general they are all good because in addition to being light and marvelously fast, they rein well and respond to punishment, without bad habits like those from here in Spain, and they breed better and stronger hooves. They have but one fault, that they are not high-steppers, and running well comes from this; but as they are low-steppers they charge better and are lighter, and fourteen years old is not an old horse.[3]

In the early days of settlement in Mexico and the American Southwest, the vaqueros tended to be of mestizo and mulatto origin. Originally, the vaqueros were often tied to one cattle baron for the entirety of their lives, but late in that same century some changes emerged. Referred to as *hombres de fuste* (saddle-tree men), *vagamundos* (drifters or vagabonds), and *forajidos* (outlaws), these men roamed the Mexican countryside on horseback, working for the highest bidder.

Known as superior horsemen, in time these men came to be called rancheros.

There were also people known as *mesteñeros* (mustangers might be a suitable English equivalent) who caught the horses that roamed the

Cowboy by J. R. McFarren, artist c.1886.

American Great Plains and the San Joaquin Valley of California, and later ventured into Nevada's Great Basin. Again, there are regional differences that come into play with the vaqueros and mesteñeros. Regardless of whether they first came into California, Texas, New Mexico, or other locations, their heritage influenced the cowboy as we think of him (or a cowgirl) today. With the conclusion of the Mexican–American War in 1848, many Anglos flooded the Texas region. Many of them took over former Mexican ranches, retaining the invaluable vaqueros. The later discovery of gold led many people of all backgrounds westward into the California goldfields in 1849. Then came the Colorado gold rush of 1859 and the beginnings of the Civil War in 1861. All of this meant migration happened full tilt in the American territories on a massive scale, blending cultures and horse-handling skills to match the climate, the terrain, and the horses available.

Some historians estimate that up to one-quarter of the cowboy population were African Americans.

After the Civil War, many vaqueros traveled north. The end of the Civil War marks the birth of the stereotypical American age of the cowboy. Riders accompanied the trail drives that pointed the Texas cattle north to feed the gold camps and northern settlements, along with their trusty horses.

THE COWBOYS

Between 1866 and 1886, some forty thousand cowboys drove more than nine million cattle from Texas to railroad centers five hundred miles north in Kansas. During that period, the beef industry grew so large that 44 percent of all the land in the United States was devoted to raising cattle. Throughout the sixteenth, seventeenth, and eighteenth centuries, the vaqueros tended these ranches, creating and perfecting the aspects of cattle raising that would come to mark the American cowboy's way of life.

Large-scale ranching began in the United States immediately after the end of the Civil War in 1865. Many of the American cowboys were veterans of that conflict. The clothes they wore, the equipment they used, the techniques they employed, and many of the terms they used were all taken from the vaqueros. Most of the cowboys' horses were descendants of the animals that the Spanish had brought to the New World. Cattle raising required a large string of horses. In the late spring, cowboys would capture local wild horses to take back to the ranch, where skilled horsemen trained them for use on the ranch.[4]

The American cowboy came in many different varieties as to their backgrounds and walks of life and were as varied as the horses they rode. One of the commonalities between all of them was the respect they developed for their horses. Perhaps nothing brings the spirit of that time and their relation to their mounts more than their own words. Fortunately, some kept records of their recollections or collaborated with writers who published them decades later. One thing remains for certain: Cowboys and their horses formed a unique and often profound partnership. This is not to say that all horses were equally esteemed, displayed the same skills, or had the same personalities. In fact, different horses performed different functions. A *remuda* refers to a string of horses available for different cowboys to ride, and since all horses (and riders) are not created equal, different combinations worked better for varying tasks and needs.

Teddy "Blue" Abbott is one of the better-known cowboys of the late 1890s. Part of the reason for his prominence is that he married one of the daughters of Granville Stuart of Montana fame. That, and the man could tell a story—or several. An author named Helena Huntington Smith, who met him in 1937, acted as his partner in publishing his memoir. Abbot's accounts, which Smith recorded, spanned the years from 1871 to 1889, and covered wide swaths of territory in the American West, from Texas to Montana. Full of daring-do, Abbott recounts his life spent largely in the saddle.

One of his vignettes recalled one of his favorite horses, and how it became his, after a struggle.

One morning Bill Charlton was riding a half-broke horse, and he couldn't ride very good. The horse cut up some, and Bill got mad and spurred him. At that time they all had these Mexican spurs with long rowels and bells on them, and a long hook—the cinch hook it was called—on top of the rowel; this was to hook into them leather bands, when a horse was bucking, and keep you from being throwed. Now, Bill accidentally ran this hook into the conch ring, and it caught there, and the horse bucked him off. He would have been kicked to death in a minute. I was riding a green horse myself, but I got alongside Bill's horse and grabbed the cheek strap and throwed myself out of the saddle. But my own spur caught on the cantle, and there I was stretched out for about a second between them two horses. Then I got loose and dropped to the ground. . . .

He said, "What have I got that you want?"

I said: "Give me that little bay horse."

He said: "Hell, take a good horse." But I wanted that little bay. So he gave him to me and that was how I got little Billy—named for Bill Charlton—that was my top horse for twenty-six years.

The next day I caught him up to ride, and he showed me a thing or two. He started to buck, and first my six-shooter went, then my Winchester went, then I went, and he finished up by bucking the saddle over his head. After that, I would not have taken a million dollars for him. He was about ten years old when I got him, and was thirty-six years old when he died on this ranch of old age. He was a wonderful rope and cut horse, but I thought so much of him I never used him much, only to ride him to town."[5]

Obviously, the bond between Teddy Blue and his horse Billy ran deep.

HISTORIC HORSE DRIVES

While almost everyone knows about the great cattle drives, one of the often-overlooked aspects of western settlement and history were the horse drives. Known as "horse trailing," it proved a difficult and unusual business in many ways. Take for instance the following story about a young Danish emigrant named Henry Nelson (known as H. H.). His family left Denmark for Quebec in 1866. A year later, they made their way down to Minnesota, where his father purchased a farm. Henry was sixteen when he took a herd of cattle up to Winnipeg, Manitoba, working for Sam Spencer for five summers. Spencer would later become one of Montana's largest cattle operators in the Maria's country along the Maria River. During those five summers, H. H. gained the experience needed to become a tough and resourceful trail driver.[6]

In 1881, for whatever reason, H. H. was in Bismarck, North Dakota, along with a Norwegian friend called, somewhat contradictorily, "Swede." Regardless, H. H. and Swede were wandering around Bismarck when Henry caught wind of a man named Robins looking for someone to trail horses to Montana. Their paths crossed at a restaurant, where young Nelson was able to convince Mr. Robbins of his ability. It didn't hurt that Robbins knew his former employer, Sam Spencer. Robbins decided to give Nelson a chance. Truth be told, he may not have had that many options to hire. He explained that he had sold a band of "American" mares along with some stallions to the Larabie brothers at Deer Lodge. Not to mention that trailing the mares and stallions comprised only part of the job description. The horses needed to be saddle-broken as well for the simple reason that rideable horses brought in more money upon delivery.

It was, indeed, a long way from Bismarck to Deer Lodge.

In an article written by Nelson's granddaughter, she claimed that "Recruiting a crew wasn't easy. The likely looking ones sang the same refrain, 'Horse trailing? Not me. Went with a horse herd once. And you're bringing stallions along? No thanks.'"[7]

The journey to Deer Lodge didn't pass easily, nor was it uneventful. The Dakotas and Montana in 1881 were home to American Indians, bears, bad weather, horse thieves, and anything else of danger one could imagine. At the banks of the Little Missouri River, the party encountered skinned and rotting buffalo carcasses. Assailed by the stench and the unfamiliar sight—the horses stampeded before the trail hands were able to rectify the situation.

They ran into all sorts of characters, but the most dangerous of the long journey was when a bear caused a stampede, and a young trailhand called "Punk" and a stallion were killed. This was followed in quick succession by a shale slide that buried the body of the young man. In addition, several of the horses scattered, and it took the riders two days to round up the horses that they could find. Nine horses had to be shot due to the severity of their wounds received in the stampede, and the men never did find thirty-two. At the end of the gather, 268 horses were accounted for, with one less rider.

The men delivered the horses to the Larabies and were paid their agreed amount.[8]

Nelson settled in Montana.

Of course, horse trailing took place throughout the west. California had plenty of horses to sell, and their riders would trail them eastward to where the markets were. One rather remarkable account without details claimed, "Five thousand California horses, from Kerr, Tulare county, California, are being driven overland, bound for Denver."[9]

Considering the difficulties that trailing three hundred horses caused, the extraordinary total of five thousand head hopefully was an enthusiastic exaggeration at the time.

EARLY HORSE BREEDERS AND MASS SALES FOR WAR

As soon as parts of the West opened for settlement, the need for horse breeders and sellers quickly followed. One of the more notable horse ranchers was known by several sobriquets, including the Queen of Diamonds and the Horse Queen of the West. She was the only daughter of the Wilkins family, owners of the Wilkins Horse Company. A massive operation that owned close to ten thousand horses in Owyhee County, Idaho, theirs was believed the largest herd owned by one single family in the West. When the ranch operations passed from the parents to their children, Kittie became its boss. It is often claimed that she was the only woman at the time whose sole occupation was selling horses.[10]

Beyond her glittering and successful career and reputation witnessed by her nicknames, Kittie's life started out as the child of emigrants. Her parents named her Katherine Caroline Wilkins, born in Jacksonville, Oregon, in 1857. Her family moved to Florence, Idaho, to follow a gold rush in 1862. The family underwent a series of moves, but in the 1860s, upon Laura Wilkins' father's death, her mother received a legacy. From those proceeds, the family bought a small herd of "Oregon" mares. Oregon horses were descended from American Indian breeds and footsore emigrant stock (often referred to as American horses). These horses bred, and their offspring "Oregon" horses came to be known as a hearty breed well-suited to their western climate. In the 1870s, the Wilkins ran a herd south of Boise City.

It becomes apparent from a series of moves around Idaho made before settling down in Bruneau, Idaho, that Kitty's father J. R. had ranching in his blood. The Wilkins opened up a large spread called the Wilkins Island Ranch, located at the fork of the Bruneau River near Jarbidge Mountain. Their holdings strung along the Snake River and into Elko County, Nevada. Their range extended seventy-five miles from their ranch headquarters, stretching into the Owyhee Mountains.

Apparently, her father also ran a successful operation with several thousand head of cattle and horses. As an excellent horsewoman, Kitty favored the equines. At the height of the ranch's breeding program, it is believed that the Wilkins' operation ran ten thousand head of horses.

As the story goes, when her father took young Kitty back east to a horse market, she became enamored with the business of raising and selling horses. She traveled with her father from that point forward to his horse markets and sales. She developed her own marketing plan, and the attractive young woman found she was successful in selling horses—more so than her father. In the 1880s, Kittie imported blooded stallions from the Midwest and the east to breed with her Oregon mares.[11]

At some point in time, Kittie began buying Clydesdale, Percheron, Morgan, Norman, and Hambletonian stallions. She claimed after that point that there were "No native Oregon or Spanish horses"[12] on her ranch. Whether this remained strictly true or not, when Great Britain entered the Boer War in South Africa in 1899, the British army came calling for western horses. In 1900, Kittie Wilkins supplied them by selling eight thousand head to a buyer or dealer in Kansas City. This single sale was reckoned to be 7 percent of the total number of American-supplied horses and the largest sale supplied by a single rancher.[13]

Other ranchers and suppliers throughout the western United States also supplied war horses to the British government for both the Boer

Cowboys eating out on the range, 1880–1910.
LIBRARY OF CONGRESS.

War and World War I—sales were documented in Idaho, Wyoming, and Montana. The documented numbers supplied are 109,878 horses and 81,524 mules.[14]

The following World War I account (although somewhat lengthy) paints a vivid picture of the manner in which the livestock were sold and bound into service. The *Sheridan (Wyoming) Post* describes:

INSPECTING WAR HORSES FOUR HUNDRED PUR-CHASED AT POLO RANCH. GOVERNMENT STAMP Placed on the animals that pass muster and are bought for service. The center of the horse-loving population of Northern Wyoming, the first two days of this week, was the Polo ranch near Big Horn where Messers McNeal and Boze. Official horse inspectors and buyers for the British government, were purchasing mounts for the army operating in Europe. . . .

The Inspection opened early Monday morning, and was completed late Tuesday afternoon. During that time, approximately 400 head of horses were purchased from probably twice as many presented to the Inspectors. The requirements of the British government are strict, and it was the cream of the equine population of the Sheridan country which there involuntarily enlisted for service with the allies. The first requirement of the purchase was that the animal be sound in every particular; the second that he be of the correct height, that is fifteen hands or better, the third, that he be between the ages of five and nine, that is a mature animal but with several years of usefulness before him. The fourth, that he be of a dark color, not easily distinguishable by the enemy, and a good, free, square-gaited traveler. Horses meeting these requirements passed readily. They were led at once to an improvised branding chute where they received the stamp of the British government. Those, which failed to meet the requirements were turned in the opposite direction galloped away with as many manifestations of joy as if they realized what they had escaped.

The horses which were accepted and purchased were shod before being taken away from the Polo ranch, a large force of expert horsemen from Sheridan going to the ranch Wednesday morning for the job no small one, as anyone will realize who has even attempted to fasten on a horseshoe. As soon as ready the horses will be loaded into cars at Sheridan and shipped to Canada where they will be thrown in with other bunches, larger and smaller purchased elsewhere, and prepared for shipment across the water. They will go immediately into the service of the army.

The horses purchased by the inspectors were divided into four classes and the price paid depends upon the class. The order. Determined by the size and build of the animals was: Artillery, light gun. Cavalry and cobs. Purchase in the two latter classes greatly outnumbered the other classes Local horsemen are of the opinion that, should the war continue for any length of time. the requirements of the army buyer will be cut appreciably and that many horses now rejected will then be accepted at prices as good as are now being paid. Proceedings . . . were relieved of tedium at frequent intervals by the efforts of none-too-well broken horses to disqualify themselves for army services by throwing their riders. . . . When the horse was properly subdued, he went the way of his brethren, to be accepted or rejected as the case might be. All horses were supposed to be broken but there were some that barely came within that definition. Practically all the horses offered belonged to Moncreiffe Bros., Wallop and Walsh and had been purchased by them or their agents in all parts of Northern Wyoming.[15]

Each state and region had its own horse breeders, and obviously the size of the operations and the quality of the breeders varied. And the love of horses was not limited to ranchers. Adolph Zang of Denver, Colorado, was a noted brewer and industrialist in mining. However, he was also a horseman at heart. In 1885, Zang purchased nearly four thousand acres in what is now Broomfield. The ranch was popularly known as the Zang Ranch, but actually its proper name was the Elmwood Stock Farm. After spending much time contemplating what he would consider to be the ideal Percheron for Colorado, he began his breeding operations in 1893. He purchased seven mares and a remarkably high-class stallion from France, a two-year-old named Champagne 51743, for the princely sum of five thousand dollars (which is the equivalent of $169,850 in

Inspecting horses for overseas wars.

today's dollars). By 1910, Champagne would be considered the most valuable stud horse in the world.[16]

Zang's Percherons were considered a hardier horse able to breathe at altitude. Several Zang stallions were sold to Summit County ranchers where they suited the needs of the high country.

According to the classic work *A History of the Percheron Horse* by Dr. Alvin Howard Sanders and Wayne Dinsmore in 1917:

> The greatest progress in this state, however, has been made in grading up the native range horses, in which (Zang's) Percherons have been the leading part. The free use of Percheron stallions on the native horses in Colorado has increased the size, improved the symmetry and confor-mation, and brought about such improvement in the general type and quality of the horses that they are worth from two to three times as much as the native stock from which they sprang.[17]

Horse breeding could be a profitable business, as many of the large breed-ers evidenced.

FAMOUS WESTERN SADDLE MAKERS AND SADDLE-MAKING TOWNS

People are particular about their saddles, and riders have their favorites. Certain towns built their reputations of hosting a variety of skilled and sought-after saddle makers. Two that come to mind are Miles City, Montana, and Pueblo, Colorado, both located along the old Texas cattle trails. Charles Goodnight owned a spread near Pueblo, and the old Texas trails up into eastern Montana provided a fine business start.

The saddlery reputation of Miles City rides on into the present.

Ask many residents of the town, and they will tell you that Miles City revolves around horses. Some even claim that Miles City "boasted more saddle shops than any place on earth,"[18] which may or may not be true. Like Pueblo, most of the saddle shops in the twenty-first century have closed their doors and ceased operations with the notable excep-tion of the Miles City Saddlery, which remains the only place to buy an original Coggshall. In fact, some of the saddles kept on display in the museum portion of the shop are over one hundred years old. The first famous saddle maker was Al Furstnow, who began his business in August 1894. Coggshall bought into his business as a partner in December of that same year. While Coggshall was not a saddler, it "was under his guidance that the Montana Saddle Tree was perfected." The partnership split in 1899, with Coggshall forming the immediate predecessor of today's Miles City Saddlery.

Most saddleries made four to six saddles per week. When World War I broke out, two dozen men were employed, and production increased to 1,937. Saddle making has always been a laborious process, taking two to three weeks per saddle. The length of time required depends upon the intricacy of carving the features.

Some of Miles City's most prestigious and famous saddle makers include the following:

Pioneer Saddlery & Harness Shop: 1850s to 1879

Goettlich & Debord: 1880 to 1881

Moran Brothers: 1884 to 1887

Robbins & Lenoir: 1891 to 1894

Furstnow & Coggshall: 1894 to 1899

George E. Robbins: 1895 to 1902

Al Furstnow Saddlery: 1899 to 1982

C.E. Coggshall Saddlery: 1899 to 1909

Miles City Saddlery: 1909 to present

Pete Verbeck's Saddle Shop: 1946 to 1976

Carl Wilson's Saddlery: 1961 to 1983

Nunn & Thibault Saddle Shop: 1978 to 1984

T-Bone Saddle Shop: 1984 to present[19]

Pueblo, Colorado, is another formidable saddle town, with its own past to boast about. Pueblo claims it was known as the saddle-making capital of the world between 1870 and 1921.[20] In Pueblo, it wasn't just the cowboys and the proximity to the Goodnight Loving Trail that created the demand, but also the nearby coal and silver mines. Harnesses were in demand by mining operations, as well as local farms and cattle ranching. R. T. Frazier is probably considered the most famous of the Pueblo saddle makers, but the first documented saddlery in Pueblo was owned by Cornelius Joseph Hart around 1867. Hart was followed by S. C. Gallup starting in 1870. It was Gallup who developed what would become known as the highly collectible "Pueblo saddle," boasting a thick and sturdy structure.

Frazier was founded in 1898, and the business employed more than fifty saddle and harness craftsmen. In 1917, Frazier was reportedly the

Robert Thompson "R. T." Frazier and his wife Katherine Rose "Kittie" Henley.
PUEBLO COUNTY HISTORICAL SOCIETY.

largest maker of "cowboy saddles" in the country.[21] Frazier remained in business until 1958.

Fred McConnell started out working for Gallup, Frazier, and the Flynn companies before starting his own company called Mack's Saddlery. His business, however, was destroyed by fire in 1989.

Many saddle makers faced increased competition from national stores such as Sears Roebuck & Co. and western specialty stores which carried saddles, and the sun set on the day of the custom, locally made saddle in the 1980s.

THE HORSE AS A SYMBOL OF HOPE

The city of Pueblo was devastated by a massive flood on June 5, 1921. Between 150 and 250 people died, and the damages were assessed at over $358 million dollars in today's valuations. The saddler R. T. Frazer had a large, life-sized dapple gray papier-mâché horse with real horsehair in his business as a display. Like so much else in Pueblo, that horse was swept away in the flood waters. But here's where the story gets good. High up in a cottonwood tree near Avondale, Colorado (about fifteen miles downstream from Pueblo), an object was lodged in the branches.

It was the horse from Frazier's store, and miraculously, only his ears were damaged![22]

Kittie Frazier (R. T.'s wife) mended the ears when the horse was lowered down to ground and returned. Now christened "Lucky," the horse's construction contained a barrel in the belly, which helped the buoyancy, and his papier-mâché construction reportedly contained a fair amount of hemp, which help it survive the water and battering.

The horse remained in the saddlery until 1958, when the doors closed.

Lucky is now a treasured display in Pueblo's Southern Colorado Heritage Museum, much to everyone's delight.

NOTES
1. Lakshmi Gandhi, "How Mexican Vaqueros Inspired the American Cowboy," *History*, August 17, 2023, https://www.history.com/news/mexican-vaquero-american-cowboy.

2. Lakshmi Gandhi, "How Mexican Vaqueros Inspired the American Cowboy," *History*, August 17, 2023, https://www.history.com/news/mexican-vaquero-american-cowboy.

1

3. Bernardo Vargas Machuca, *The Indian Militia and Description of the Indies*, Durham, NC: Duke University Press, 2008, 190.

4. American Quarter Horse Association, "The Cowboy's Horse," https://www.aqha.com/-/the-cowboy-s-horse-1.

5. E.C. "Teddy Blue" Abbott and Helena Huntington Smith, *We Pointed Them North: Recollections of a Cowpuncher*, Norman, OK: University of Oklahoma Press, 1986, 43–44.

6. Elizabeth Greenfield, "A Horse Drive to Montana Territory, 1881," *Montana: The Magazine of Western History* 13, no. 3 (1963): 18–33.

7. Greenfield, "A Horse Drive," 20.

8. Long Riders Guild Academic Foundation, "Historic Horse Rides," http://www.lrgaf.org/journeys/drives.htm.

9. *The Rocky Mountain News* (Daily), "News Summary," volume 12, May 10, 1871, https://www.coloradohistoricnewspapers.org/?a=d&d=RMD18710510-01.2.15&srpos=8&e=-------en-20--1-byDA-img-txIN%7ctxCO%7ctxTA-%22California+horses%22-ARTICLE------0------.

10. National Endowment of the Humanities, "Woman of the West: Horse Queen of Idaho," https://www.neh.gov/humanities/2012/marchapril/statement/woman-the-west.

11. Philip A. Homan, "Meeting Miss Kittie: My Friendship with Kittie Wilkins the Horse Queen of Idaho," Rural Women's Studies, Pocatello, ID: Idaho State University, September 16, 2015, https://ruralwomensstudies.wordpress.com/2015/09/16/meeting-miss-kittie-my-friendship-with-kittie-wilkins-the-horse-queen-of-idaho.

12. Erin Turner (Ed.), *Cowgirls: Stories of Trick Riders, Sharp Shooters, and Untamed Women*, Guildford, CT: TwoDot Books, 2009, 13.

13. Bureau of Land Management, "Kittie Wilkins: Idaho's Horse Queen," https://www.blm.gov/blog/2021-03-10/kittie-wilkins-idahos-horse-queen.

14. Philip A. Hoffman, "American Horses for the South African War, 1899–1902," https://www.environmentandsociety.org/arcadia/american-horses-south-african-war-1899-1902.

15. *Sheridan Post*, November 27, 1914, https://sheridanmedia.com/news/91988/sheridan-county-horses-go-to-war.

16. *Daily Camera (Boulder, CO)*, https://www.dailycamera.com/2023/01/01/in-retrospect-zang-ranch-was-famous-for-percheron-horses.

17. Alvin Howard Sanders and Wayne Dinsmore, *A History of the Percheron Horse*, Chicago, Breeders Gazette Print, 1917, 464.

18. Matt Villano, "Miles City Saddlery is as Smooth as Leather," *Montana Living*, March 10, 2016, https://www.montanaliving.com/blogs/mercantile/112959237-miles-city-saddlery-is-smooth-as-leather.

19. Villano, "Miles City Saddlery."

20. "Pueblo: Former Saddle Center," *Pueblo Cheiftain*, January 15, 2012, https://www.chieftain.com/story/lifestyle/2012/01/15/pueblo-former-saddle-center/8416123007.

21. Gianna Lisec, "Saddles a Big Part of Pueblo History," *Pueblo Chieftain*, October 5, 2011, https://www.chieftain.com/story/news/2011/10/05/saddles-big-part-pueblo-history/8723934007.

22. Sarah Wilson, "The Legend of Lucky the Papier-Mache Horse that Survived Pueblo's Great Flood of 1921," *The Pueblo Chieftain*, June 3, 2021, https://www.chieftain.com/story/news/2021/06/03/pueblo-flood-1921-survivor-lucky-papier-mache-horse/7495938002.

CHAPTER 6

DARING WESTERN RIDES

Near Wyoming's Green River. Men like these might have made heroic dashes or rides.
WYOMING STATE ARCHIVES, CARTER COLLECTION.

DARING RIDES REQUIRED HEROIC HORSES—ALTHOUGH HISTORICALLY, most of the accolades are cast in the direction of the rider. Since each account is separate and a matter of life and death, this chapter goes chronologically so as not to place one accomplishment in a stronger light than another. And as all distance riders know, such long rides are tremendously taxing and difficult for both the rider and, especially, their mount. Unlike the western movies, not all those missions forcing the cross-country runs succeeded in their desired outcomes, although the extreme efforts of man or horse cannot be faulted. The bottom line remains indisputable—distances were far, the terrain was rugged, and the environment and its inhabitants could easily be hostile. So much came down to chance.

Remarkably, two separate events involved riders whose last names were Haslam. Both were born in England.

James Holt Haslam has largely been ignored by history due to the circumstances surrounding his ride and the smack of infamy. In 1857, an event known as the Utah War was in full cry. Although this time in history may not be well-known to people outside of Utah, it marked a contest between the Mormon settlers in the then Utah Territory and the US government. Having faced serious persecution in other states, the Latter Day Saints were fearful that the large US Army force stationed within the Utah Territory had been sent to either annihilate or, at the very least, curb the adherents' religious practices. At what would be viewed as the height of flaring tensions, the Baker-Fancher band (or train) of emigrants from Missouri and Arkansas crossed through the territory, heading toward California. Rumors flew about their behavior toward the Mormons that likely played into their fates.

Stopping to rest at a place called the Mountain Meadows about thirty-five miles southwest of Cedar City, the travelers were to be involved in the event that became known as the Mountain Meadows Massacre. It was there that the Utah Militia, together with Paiute allies, attacked the resting party and killed between 120 and 150 people.

This is the dark stain on Utah's history.

All emigrants were killed except for young children under the approximate age of seven. Women and older children were not spared.

James Holt Haslam was born in Bolton, Lancashire, England, in 1825, the son of John Haslam and Alice Young. At the age of eighteen, he joined the Latter Day Saints and left home, traveling to first New Orleans, then on to Cincinnati, and finally on to Nauvoo, Illinois, before traveling west. His family joined him from England and secured what was needed to make their journey to Utah. Along the way, cholera struck. According to some sources, it seems that James lost most of his family, along with his first wife, whose name is unknown. James and his remaining family reached Salt Lake City, but in 1853 they were called by the church to settle in the remote location of Cedar City to help in the iron industry.[1]

The Utah Militia (also referred to as the Nauvoo Legion) in Cedar City was led by a man named Colonel Isaac C. Haight, who acted as the commander. Reportedly, the emigrants tried to purchase supplies and were refused, as they had been through a good portion of Utah. Threats were made by the emigrants saying they might take the supplies by force, or words to that effect.[2] A great debate arose around whether to attack them. Overwhelmingly, the prevailing preference was for attack. However, not all assembled agreed and were reluctant to pursue such a drastic course of action. As a means of compromise, or to mollify the dissenters, Haight agreed that the Nauvoo Militia would apprise Brigham Young of their debate. He appointed James Holt Haslam to carry the dispatch to the Latter Day Saints president, informing him of the impending course of action. That dispatch contained the one chance to prevent slaughter and has long been lost to time.

Regardless, on September 10, 1857, a communication was handed to the young rider who undertook the three-hundred-mile journey to Salt Lake City. By many accounts, the attack on the emigrant train had already started.

Armed with a letter stating Haslem's/the militia's business with the request that local bishops furnish fresh horses as needed, he set out.

When he finally reached President Young with the letter, Young responded:

> In regard to emigration trains passing through our settlements, we must not interfere with them until they are first notified to keep away. You must not meddle with them. The Indians we expect will do as they please but you should try and preserve good feelings with them. There are no other trains going south that I know of. . . . If those who are there will leave let them go in peace.[3]

Haslem galloped back with Brigham Young's response, but the letter arrived two days too late on September 13, 1857.

The Baker-Fancher party had been obliterated.

Investigations into the slaughter began in 1857, but the process proved slow and drawn out. Eventually the inquiries were placed on hold, delayed by the Civil War. In 1874, some of the participants were arrested. In 1884, twenty-seven years after the event, an inquiry came to light where James Haslam, the man who rode to notify Brigham Young, testified.

The formatting and punctuation are unique, but an excerpt of his testimony is as follows with the original punctuation:

What kind of horse did you start on.

A spanish horse.

Please state as to its fleetness.

I could not state as to that.

How long did it take you to arrive at Parowan?

I could not state exactly, might be two hours.

What was the distance?

Between eighteen and twenty miles.

Did you proceed on the same horse from there?

Yes sir, to Beaver.

Do you know what time you arrived at Beaver?

. . . about nine o'clock . . .

Did you change horses at Beaver?

Yes, sir[4]

From Beaver to Filmore, Haslam rode the same horse. There is where he hit a delay. He reached Filmore slightly before daylight, but the bishop had gone hunting, taking his horses with him. Haslam could do nothing but wait for his return, since the horse he rode was too exhausted to continue. Then, when the bishop finally arrived, Haslam was provided a horse that could "only go ten miles." To make matters worse, they didn't have another horse when he stopped at the settlement of Holden.

The people in Holden actually had to send back to Filmore for another horse.

At three o'clock in the morning the fresh(-ish) horse arrived, and Haslam proceeded to Salt Creek or Nephi. Then he traveled to Payson and on to Provo. Next, he rode to American Fork and finally on to Salt Lake City. Under examination, it was determined that it took Haslem around sixty hours to reach Salt Lake City. Haslam reckoned that fifteen to twenty hours were lost due to "stoppages." (This all illustrates the fact that horses were not always readily available, of the same caliber, or merely waiting around to be pressed into service.)

Haslam hand-delivered the message to Brigham Young and was told by the president to rest and to sleep, and to return to his office at four o'clock that same afternoon. The earlier cross-examination continued:

Were you there at the time he mentioned for you to come?

I was.

What took place then?

He told me to start and not to spare horseflesh, but to go down there just as quick as possible.

There were more questions as to whether Haslam read the message. He did not.

Resuming:

About how long were you on the road and taking the message down to Cedar City?

About the same as I was coming up, as near as I can think.

What did Mr. Haight say to you when you handed him the message or answer and he read it?

He said, "Too late, too late." The massacre was over before I got home.[5]

Another Haslam had a different difficult ride.

Born in London, England, in 1840, the daring account of Robert "Pony Bob" Haslam's Pony Express career is known to many. Pony Bob came to the United States as part of the Great Migration. A member of the Latter Day Saints, Bob made his way to the Utah Territory, as did so many. Strangely enough, accounts of Bob Haslem's life don't vary much from one account to another, and they *really* don't vary on his marathon ride. But here goes.

Once, when Nevada was a part of Utah Territory, Haslam met a man named Bolivar Roberts—one of Superintendent Ficklin's deputies.[6] As that name is likely not familiar to many, Benjamin Ficklin was high up in the organization as the supervisor of the Pony Express' entire route. Bolivar Roberts hired Bob to assist with the construction of some of the stations in that region as the Pony Express' mail service started operations. He kept Haslam on as a rider, assigning him to Friday's Station near Lake Tahoe. Pony Bob's route typically ran between Friday's and Fort Churchill. On May 7, 1860, an incident at the Williams Station in Carson Valley, Nevada, set off what is known as both the Paiute and the Pyramid Lake War. Williams Station provided a saloon, a stage stop, and a general store combined. Although, once again, details are scarce and uncertain, there are multiple versions of what might have provoked the violence. One version had to do with the mistreatment of a Paiute woman at the hands of four white men. The Paiute woman, accompanied by an older man, was let go. However, Bannock, Paiute, or Shoshone men returned, forced the offenders into the station house, and burned the place down around them. Another version involves a horse trade or sale gone bad, culminating with a Paiute man being bitten by the station dog, and yet another involves two captive Paiute children tied up and held underground.[7] While there are many variations on that story (and none of them paint a favorable picture of the owners of Williams Station), most versions of the sordid tale agree that four to five white men were found dead. Some accounts have the building being burned down around them, and all that remained were smoldering ruins. Other accounts have them murdered and mutilated, but unburned. If one believes the unburned version, as luck would have it, the owner J. O. Williams was away when the building was torched and returned to find his two brothers' mutilated bodies along with three murdered patrons of the establishment.

None of this involved Pony Bob, other than he had a ride to make and a circuit to run.

Bob started out on his regular run from Friday's. When he reached Carson City, he was surprised to find that there was no relay horse waiting for him. He learned that it had been requisitioned by the state militia to go after the Paiutes in the budding war.

Bob had no choice but to ride on, mounted on his same tired horse.

Upon reaching Buckland's Station, he found the relief rider, Johnson Richardson, refusing to get in the saddle. Richardson declared himself unwilling to make the already dangerous journey due to the unfolding hostilities.

Station Manager W. C. Marley offered Bob fifty dollars to ride the next leg himself. Pony Bob took the money.

Mounting the fresh horse, he rode on to the Cold Springs station and further on to Smith's Creek. When all was said and done, Pony Bob likely rode 160 to 170 miles along the trail one way.

At Smith's Creek, Bob mercifully slept a few hours before rousing himself (or being roused) to take the mochila from the westbound rider. He rode back the way he came, his first destination Cold Springs. When he reached the station that he had passed through the day before, he found a scene of devastation. The station keeper was killed, the building burned, and all the horses either taken or run off.

He had no choice but to keep riding.

When he reached the Sand Springs Station, he told Montgomery Maze, the station master, what he had seen back down the trail.

After hearing Haslam's account, Maze didn't need hard convincing to join him in leaving. Together they rode to Carson Sink on May 13. There they found that station barricaded by about fifteen jittery men, all understandably concerned about battles with American Indians.

Pony Bob rode on. Hopefully, he had a change of horses.

He returned to Buckland's where he began the regular portion of his run, back through Carson City and heading toward Friday's Station. Just like nothing at all had transpired.

It was, on many levels, one hell of a ride.

In 1866, another series of hostilities smoldered: Red Cloud's War, this time involving the Lakota Nation. Much has been written about the Fetterman Fight, and more especially the bravado behind the claim "with 80 men, I could ride through the whole Sioux Nation." (Reportedly said by Captain William, J. Fetterman, there is no proof that he actually uttered those now-famous words.) While that claim might have been made up at the turn of the last century in the 1900s, the grandiosity behind that statement clearly wasn't.

In a nutshell, the Bozeman Trail that cut through Wyoming and Montana crossed through the best hunting lands of the Lakota, who had earlier pushed out the Crow with their numbers a might. A man named John Bozeman, in an attempt to find a quicker way to lead wagon trains to the Montana goldfields, cut right through the heart of Lakota territory. While Bozeman's new route shaved off precious travel time, it came at the risk of death or at least the risk of provoking hostilities.

Forts were established along that new route ostensibly to protect the settlers, but really they were built to protect the interests of the US government. In the years immediately after the Civil War, the government desperately needed the gold that the Montana fields could provide.

Fetterman's arrogance, according to the accepted story, led to grand recklessness on December 21, 1866, when he disobeyed Commander Carrington's direct orders to relieve a woodcutting detail under attack west of the fort, bring it in safely to the pinery blockhouses, and, above all else, refrain from crossing Lodge Trail Ridge in pursuit of the American Indians. Ignorantly and defiantly, Fetterman led his command from Fort Phil Kearny in pursuit of a decoy party of ten Lakotas and Cheyennes over the forbidden ridge into an ambush of fifteen hundred to two thousand Lakota, Cheyenne, and Arapaho warriors. The warriors annihilated the captain and his command in a short, brutal action.[8]

The hero in this story is a civilian rider named John "Portugee" Phillips. He was born Manuel Felipe Cardoso in the Azores and spoke Portuguese as his first language, hence the nickname. He came to the United States by ship to hunt for gold. When that didn't materialize, he cast around the west and ended up as a civilian water hauler at Fort Kearney.

It was the evening of December 21, 1866. Fort Phil Kearney was in a desperate situation, as the annihilation of at least one-quarter of the fort's fighting force had occurred just that afternoon. The fear was that two thousand to three thousand warriors remained in the vicinity, anxious to rid themselves of the fort and its intruding inhabitants once and for all. The situation inside the fort was so grim that plans were made to sequester the women and children inside the fort's ammunition magazine—should the fort be overrun, the powder kegs would be fired, blowing them all to smithereens, lest they fall into the warriors' hands.

That evening, a wiry, soft-spoken man with a Portuguese accent stepped forward and volunteered to make the dangerous ride to Fort Laramie for assistance. Along with another rider named Daniel Dixon, each man received three hundred dollars to risk the arduous journey. Fort Laramie, located 263 miles away, was all but unreachable in the treacherous winter conditions. By nightfall, the mercury hovered at zero, and was still falling.[9]

Phillips led Commander Carrington's Thoroughbred horse—a steed named Dandy—into the mouth of a blizzard that night. What is known is that one and a half days later, the two riders made it to Fort Reno having averaged less than two miles per hour, due to conditions. At

Fort Reno, the two men were joined by a third rider, Robert Bailey, who accompanied them to Horseshoe Station, near present-day Glendo, Wyoming. There they sent a telegraph that, for some reason, the Fort Laramie operator discounted.

Portugee Phillips pressed on—this time alone.

Some forty miles to the southeast, he stumbled into Fort Laramie's parade ground to hand-deliver his dispatches to the commander. He arrived as a full-dress Christmas ball was underway, the dancing officers and ladies enjoying the candlelight and laughter. Some accounts have him delivering his message to a soldier outside. Another version has Portugee entering the festivities.

Captain David Gordon, a participant in the dance, was surely understating their reaction when he recalled, "The dress of the man, and at this hour looking for the commanding officer, made a deep impression upon the officers and others that happened to get a glimpse of him and consequently, and naturally too, excited their curiosity as to his mission in this strange garb."[10]

Regardless, Phillips croaked out the stunning news of Fetterman's slaughter, and that Fort Phil Kearney quite possibly lay under siege.

There are conflicting accounts whether the brave horse Dandy survived the ordeal, but what is known is that it took Portugee a while to recover from his frigid and taxing ordeal.

The siege of Fort Phil Kearney never materialized.

The Bozeman Trail and Forts Reno, Phil Kearney, and C. F. Smith closed to civilian traffic in 1867 due to frequent harassment and hostilities. Phillips would continue to work for the US Army as a mail carrier in 1867. He later recounted a tale of another desperate trip: "In April he reported that 15 Sioux warriors had surrounded him en route. 'Without aid of my faithful horse and good revolver,' he only half-joked, 'I would have lost my hair, the part of my body I feel most anxious about on the prairie.'"[11]

Joking aside, horses were a serious matter, and perhaps none more cared for than by members of the Ute tribe. A fiercely horse-loving culture, they were moved to the reservation after the Treaty of 1868 was signed by most of the Ute bands. This reduced the Ute territory from approximately fifty-six million acres to about eighteen million acres and created agencies on the Los Pinos River and another on the White River. The second half of the 1870s was characterized by anger, frustration, and tragedy as the various Ute bands adjusted to difficult and unfamiliar living conditions.[12]

It was into this simmering period of upheaval that a pious and unyielding man named Nathanial Meeker received the appointment as Indian Agent to the White River Agency. A dreamer of grand social experiments, historically he failed at most of his undertakings. Now he took the chance to turn his attention toward converting the Utes from a nomadic, horse-loving people into farmers. Meeker's appointment was partly due to his experience with irrigated farming in Greeley, and he quickly noticed that the agency buildings were on land ill-suited for irrigation. His first order was to move the agency downstream on the White River, directly onto a pasture where the Utes grazed and raced horses.[13]

The final straw came when he learned that a Ute leader named Johnson was growing crops to feed his racing horses. Meeker, upon hearing of the purpose of those crops, ordered that field plowed under.

Meeker called for assistance from the US Army when Johnson and another Ute assaulted Meeker over the incident. When other bands of Ute noticed the incoming troops, they warned that troops entering the reservation would be interpreted as a declaration of war.

Here is where the livery owner Joe Rankin comes in. His business, and that of his two brothers—a sheriff and a jailer—was situated in Rawlins, Wyoming. "Joe, a stout, quiet, Pennsylvanian of thirty-four had been a soldier, an oil roustabout north of Pittsburgh, a freighter in the Sioux country, a gold miner at Deadwood, Central City and Hahn's Peak."[14] Not to mention that he was a "freighter, White River mail carrier and a founder of the Scottish Rite Masons."[15]

He could also ride a horse.

The Meeker family settled into life at the agency, where one of the main pastimes involved watching the races at Johnson's track, including Meeker's own daughter Josie, Joe Rankin, among many others. In the races, "The boy jockeys rode stark naked and without bridles, arms outstretched, beating and kicking and yelling like maniacs. At the finish the ponies were apt to run away, but nobody cared. If the jockey didn't like it, he just fell off."[16]

Despite the comradery the races provided, tensions simmered.

It didn't help matters when Johnson pushed Meeker in an argument. As a result, Meeker (who may have overreacted) sent a telegram to Commissioner Haight requesting help.

I HAVE BEEN ASSAULTED BY A LEADING CHIEF, JOHNSON, FORCED OUT OF MY HOUSE AND INJURED BADLY, BUT WAS RESCUED BY EMPLOYEES. IT IS NOW REVEALED THAT JOHNSON ORIGINATED ALL THE TROUBLE STATED IN LETTER SEPT.8. HIS SON SHOT AT THE PLOUGHMAN, AND OPPOSITION TO PLOWING IS WIDE. PLOWING STOPS: LIFE OF SELF, FAMILY AND EMPLOYEES NOT SAFE: WANT PROTECTION IMMEDIATELY: HAVE ASKED GOVERNOR PITKIN TO CONFER WITH GENERAL POPE.

N.C. MEEKER.[17]

Although he wasn't seriously injured, his telegram put the war wheels in motion.

Maj. Thomas Tipton Thornburgh received orders to march. Assigned to Fort Steele, Wyoming, he and about 180 men made their way south into Colorado. Thornburgh led Lieutenant B. D. Price and Captain J. S. Payne. Nicaagat (Chief Jack) met the troops at the Yampa River and requested that just Thornburgh enter the reservation so that peaceful negotiations might be held. It is also thought that Nicaagat was assessing the strength of the troops.

Captain Payne learned through Charlie Lowry and Joe Rankin (both sometimes mail carriers) that:

The danger point to the troops for a Ute ambush on the Agency Road was the three-mile stretch through Coal Creek Canyon. It began on the south side of Yellowjacket Pass eight miles from the Milk Creek Reservation line. Its walls in spots came in close to cramp the road and the stream. The walls rose as high as a thousand feet. Ute marksmen on top had a clear view of the road and they could roll boulders down upon it. The foot of Coal Creek Canyon was near Chief Jack's big village on the White River. If the troops were attacked by day in such a trap they could be destroyed.[18]

The ins and outs of the troops' approach is lengthy, but one of the main points to note is that Joe Rankin rode on ahead and found recent campfire ashes and the Milk Creek reduced to a trickle.

The major took out his field glasses and saw approximately fifty Utes high up on the ridge. Joe Rankin trotted back to the major, shaken by what he saw. Some of the men waved, both Ute and troops, but suddenly, gunfire erupted.

Thornburgh trotted alone in the tall grass along the bank of the Milk River when a single shot fired by a Ute Sharps rifle struck him in the head, above the ear, and he fell dead.

Payne took firm command. A grass fire was lit by the Ute, and the troops lit a counter fire. But dark smoke rose in the distance as well, from the burning White River Indian Agency.

Joe Rankin alerted Payne to the compounding problems. The troops were pinned down, and water was running out.

Only two men, Joe Rankin and John Gordon, had enough familiarity with the country to find their way out for help. They both volunteered to take the risk, as did Corporal George Moquin of Company F and Corporal Edward F. Murphy of Company D. Rankin came up with the plan.

Communications were prepared by Lieutenant Price including a telegram for General Crook, which read as follows:

DUTY TO ANNOUNCE THE DEATH OF MAJOR THORNBURGH WHO FELL IN HARNESS: THE PAINFUL BUT NOT SERIOUS WOUNDING OF LT. PADDOCK AND DR. GRIMES, AND KILLING OF TEN ENLISTED MEN AND A WAGON MASTER, WITH THE WOUNDING OF ABOUT TWENTY MEN AND TEAMSTERS. I AM CORRALLED NEAR WATER, WITH ABOUT THREE FOURTHS OF MY ANIMALS KILLED . . . AND BELIEVE WE CAN HOLD OUT UNTIL RE-ENFORCEMENTS REACH US, IF THEY ARE HURRIED,

OFFICERS AND MEN BEHAVED WITH GREATEST GAL-
LENTRY. I AM ALSO SLIGHTLY WOUNDED IN TWO
PLACES.

PAYNE, COMMANDER.[19]

Messages sent, it is claimed that Payne turned the command over to
Captain Lawson and promptly fainted. He was placed in the hospital pit
with the other wounded.

At 10:30 that night, an exhausted Joe Rankin led the party up Milk
Creek. Remarkably, the four men met no Utes. At 7:00 a.m., Rankin
changed horses at Fortification Creek. He later borrowed another
horse at George Bagg's Ranch on the Little Snake. He reached Rawlins at 2:00 a.m. on Wednesday, October 1. He had ridden 160 miles
in twenty-seven and a half hours. He roused the Carbon County clerk,
and they sent the telegram. By 4:30 a.m. that same day, Colonel Wesley
Merritt began assembling the relief force.

John Gordon reached Hayden, Colorado, where he met up with
Captain Dodge, Company D of the 9th Cavalry, who was en route to
the troubles from Middle Park along with his troop of buffalo soldiers.[20]

If history all but forgot Rankin and the three other men's acts of
bravery, the US government didn't. The two corporals were awarded
Medals of Honor for gallantry in action.[21] Joe Rankin was later made US
Marshal for Wyoming by President Benjamin Harrison.

The drawn-out battle claimed the lives of fourteen US soldiers, three
army teamsters, and twenty-three Ute warriors.

THE GREAT CHADRON-TO-CHICAGO
ONE-THOUSAND-MILE RACE

Having said all that, sometimes people just ride horses long distances for
the hell of it. In 1893, it began as a private joke in Nebraska. Standing on
the balcony of the Blaine Hotel in Chadron, Jim Hartzel, in front of nine
horsemen lined up in a belligerent mood, fired off his pistol at 5:33 in the
evening on June 13. The Regimental 9th Cavalry band began to play, and
some thirty-five hundred spectators lined the streets. But these men were
true riders. They didn't gallop off, but more accurately ambled.

The nine riders were Doc Middleton (listed in the horse thief chapter and very familiar with the Nebraska Sand Hills), a man called Rattlesnake whose hatband was made of rattlesnake rattles, a stagecoach driver named John Berry, and six "cowpunchers," one of who was old Joe Gillespie at 185 pounds, and the others were Dave Douglas (a teenager), Emmett Abbott, Joe Campbell from Denver, and George Jones and Charley Smith from South Dakota. The rules were that only western cowponies could be used, and only two horses to a man. The saddles weighed thirty-five pounds, and the rider had to weigh not less than 150 pounds.

John Berry had driven stagecoaches through the Indian Wars and knew the territory well. He didn't rush and rode slowly—nearly a day behind the leaders. Dave Douglas dropped out midway through the race, having worn out one horse trying to keep up with Middleton. One of Middleton's horses went lame, but he kept going, certain of the win.

One of Rattlesnake's horses failed.

At the checkpoint in the town of Galva, Iowa, Gillespie and Stephens checked in with Berry one hour behind them.

The race was nationwide news at this point.

The riders were feted, and Gillespie, in the lead, allowed his head to get turned by being in a parade and then going to a circus! Berry and Rattlesnake passed him. In De Kalb, humane society officials rode in buggies beside each rider.

Dead tired, John Berry rode into the Chicago fairgrounds at Michigan Avenue and 22nd Street. It was exactly 9:30 in the morning.

He had covered one thousand miles in thirteen days and sixteen hours. The humane officers checked his horse, named Poison, and pronounced him in fine shape.

Western horses carried the race.[22]

No doubt that there are more stories about heroic rides not covered in this account. Both horses and riders deserve much credit for their extraordinary efforts given to cover vast distances in short amounts of time. One can't help but think that had sufficient mounts been available for John Holt Haslam's ride, historic events might have turned out differently.

Western Horse Trivia

Most average horses can travel at a gallop only two miles without fatigue and about twenty miles at a trot. A horse can usually walk without stopping for twenty-five to thirty-five miles at a steady pace.

NOTES

1. Find A Grave, "John Holt Haslam," https://www.findagrave.com/memorial /39855539/james-holt-haslam.

2. Raelyn M. Embleton, *Racial Conflict in Early Utah: Mormon, Native American, and Federal Relations*, graduate thesis, Utah State University, 2019, 23–29, https:// digitalcommons.usu.edu/cgi/viewcontent.cgi?article=2430&context=gradreports.

3. James H. Haslam, interview by S.A. Kenner, reported by Josiah Rogerson, December 4, 1884, https://digitalcommons.usu.edu/cgi/viewcontent.cgi?article=2430&context =gradreports;
Brigham Young to Isaac C. Haight, September 10, 1857.

4. Unknown, *Supplement to the Lecture on the Mountain Meadows Massacre: Important Additional Testimony Recently Received*, Salt Lake City, UT, printed at Juvenile Instruction Office, 1885, 87–91.

5. *Supplement to the Lecture on the Mountain Meadows Massacre*, 95.

6. Jim DeFelice, *West Like Lightning: The Brief, Legendary Ride of the Pony Express*, New York, NY: William Morrow, 2018, 284.

7. DeFelice, *West Like Lightning*; *Parks & Travel Magazine*, https://nationalparktraveling .com/listing/pony-bob-haslam-and-his-famous-pony-express-rides/#.

8. John H. Monnett, "The Falsehoods of Fetterman's Fight," *HistoryNet*, October 1, 2010, https://www.historynet.com/the-falsehoods-of-fettermans-fight.

9. Gene Gade, "Who Was John 'Portugee' Phillips—the Man Who Rode 263 Miles to Save Fort Phil Kearney," *HistoryNet*, December 21, 2016, https://www.historynet.com /portugee-phillips-fort-phil-kearny.

10. Gade, "Who Was John 'Portugee' Phillips."

11. Gade, "Who Was John 'Portugee' Phillips."

12. James M. Potter, "Ute History and the Ute Mountain Ute Tribe," *Colorado Encyclopedia*, https://coloradoencyclopedia.org/article/ute-history-and-the-ute-mountain-ute -tribe.

13. Colorado Encyclopedia, "The Meeker Incident," https://coloradoencyclopedia.org /article/meeker-incident.

14. Marshall Sprague, *Massacre: The Tragedy at White River*, Lincoln, NE: University of Nebraska Press, 1957, 132.

15. Sprague, *Massacre*, 133.

16. Sprague, *Massacre*, 151.

17. Marshall D. Moody, "The Meeker Massacre," *Colorado Magazine* April 1952, 96, https://www.historycolorado.org/sites/default/files/media/document/2018/ColoradoMagazine_v30n2_April1953.pdf.

18. Sprague, *Massacre*, 203.

19. Michael Robert Patterson, "Thomas Tipton Thornburgh—Major, U.S. Army," https://www.arlingtoncemetery.net/ttthornburgh.htm.

20. Elmer R. Burkey, "The Thornburgh Battle with the Utes on Milk Creek," *Colorado Magazine* May 1936, 107, https://www.historycolorado.org/sites/default/files/media/document/2018/ColoradoMagazine_v13n3_May1936.pdf.

21. US Department of Defense, "US Medal of Honor Recipients," https://valor.defense.gov/Recipients/Army-Medal-of-Honor-Recipients.

22. Robert Cantwell, "The Great 1,000 Mile Race from Chadron to Chicago!" https://vault.si.com/vault/1962/09/03/the-great-1000mile-race-from-chadron-to-chicago.

CHAPTER 7

HEROIC HORSES OF THE BATTLE OF THE LITTLE BIGHORN

Comanche, the famed "lone survivor" of Custer's Last Stand. He came to symbolize the tragedy and sparked the public's collective imagination.
LIBRARY OF CONGRESS.

One of the most momentous events in the history of the young United States, one that carries a scar to this day, remains the Battle of the Little Bighorn. The shocking annihilation of "the boy general" George Armstrong Custer's command stunned the youthfully brash and confident country. Custer was a larger-than-life persona of the time—a type of early media darling. The total obliteration of one of the West's fabled fighting forces felt surreal as the news spread and cast widespread doubts as to the fighting force's invincibility on the battlefield.

The unconceivable happened, much to the horror of the nation.

Faced with a superior fighting force, when the fateful day of June 25, 1876, ended, Lt. Col. George Armstrong Custer and his entire 7th Cavalry fighting command lay dead. Decimated by the Lakota Sioux and their allies, the defeat was stunning and sobering. The entirety of the fighting men under Custer's command lay dead. There were no survivors.

Except, the legend claims, for one lone wounded horse.

The widely accepted story and the strict truth diverge at this juncture, although that is not terribly important.

What is important is that Lt. Myles Keogh's horse was found on June 27, or perhaps on June 28. Surrounded by the carnage of the battle and seriously wounded, he remained alive, standing by the river.

Gen. Alfred Howe Terry's command arrived at the Little Bighorn on June 27, 1876. Lt. Henry J. Nowlan, a close friend of Keogh's, accompanied them on their surveillance of the battlefield. He recognized the horse without hesitation and "took him in charge."[1]

The horse's name was Comanche, and soon everyone in America would know who he was.

In truth, other horses survived the brutal battle. The majority of the equine survivors in decent condition were captured by the battle's victors as spoils of war. Those horses promptly joined Lakota and Cheyenne herds. Some may have even become a warrior's prized possession. Later mentions are made of cavalry-branded horses discovered in a Sioux encampment bearing cavalry brands from Custer's Regiment: "U. S. and 7 C.—[and] one was branded with a D 7 over the letter C."[2]

Additionally, there are mentions made of other living horses discovered on the Little Bighorn's battleground suffering from severe wounds. They were shot by the troops to put an end to their suffering. With Comanche, although badly wounded, an exception was made to his immediate dispatch due to Lieutenant Nowlan's intercession. Instead, Comanche's care became viewed or held as an almost sacred duty. Leading the wounded horse from the battlefield to the steamer *Far West* fifteen or sixteen miles away took many hours.[3] Once aboard the steamer with other wounded men, the horse was made as comfortable as possible. Again, there is lack of clarity as to where Comanche recuperated; it may have been either a livery in Bismarck or Fort Lincoln. It seems more likely that Fort Lincoln took possession of the wounded horse. Regardless of the location, Comanche, placed in a "belly band" sling, was nursed back to health under the care of veterinarian Charles Stein, blacksmith Gustave Korn, and John Burkman.[4] Thanks to their effective care, Comanche to this day is frequently credited with being the lone survivor of the battle. Although that is not strictly true, it is that "lone" status that captures the imagination like nothing else.

Whether Custer is ultimately perceived as a hero or a fool, whether his foes are viewed as noble or cruel, the war justified or needless, still the horse, a joint ally of both sides, remains a hero: "He becomes at times a link between the dead and the living, a bridge between Indian and white, between humankind and animal, between the realm of speech and that of silence."[5]

Comanche's particular identity first surfaced as belonging in a herd purchased by the US Cavalry Army Quartermaster in St. Louis on April 3, 1868. He remained corralled there with the other purchased horses. After three to four weeks, they were all placed in animal train cars headed to Fort Leavenworth in Kansas where they arrived a few days later on May 10, 1868.[6] At Fort Leavenworth, the horses were processed and branded with the "US" marking on their left shoulders, designating them as belonging to the US government. As fate would have it, the 7th Cavalry was stationed near Ellis, Kansas, 280 miles distant. During those years of early western settlement, the western part of Kansas was not the farmland of today, but instead was a dangerous and contested land. The western Kansas of the 1860s experienced violent conflicts with the inhabiting tribes of that region. Raids occurred, people died, and the cavalry was tasked with policing the area. With all the hard riding and skirmishes, the cavalry needed fresh horses known as "remounts." The brother of Lieutenant Colonel Custer, Tom W. Custer, was tasked with purchasing replacement mounts for the cavalry. He purchased forty-one horses, and one of that number was Comanche who was placed in the "remount" pool.

Lieutenant Keogh, an Irish "soldier of fortune" from County Carlow, was a dashing young officer. He served in the Civil War and went on to join the cavalry. On September 13, 1868, Keogh was a member of General Sully's expedition leaving from Fort Dodge and striking into American Indian territory. Their orders were to ride southward and to find and punish "hostiles" responsible for the vicious Kansas raids carried out earlier that year.[7] The troops found a large band of Cheyenne, Kiowas, and Comanches and engaged them near the Cimarron River. Apparently, Keogh's horse was shot out from under him, and he called for a remount. That remount obviously caught his fancy and served Keogh well.

It is claimed that Keogh's second mount, who would become know as Comanche, received an arrow wound in the right hip. The shaft broke off, and the embedded arrowhead was not discovered by Keogh until the unit returned to their temporary camp. The horse acted stoically, without reacting to the pain of his injury. When the injury was indeed discovered, the arrowhead was removed by a farrier. This account is believed to form the basis behind Comanche's naming.

While not much is known about the gelding in general, he was probably about six years old when acquired by Keogh. His origins may have been from the plains of Oklahoma or Texas—in fact that seems probable—but can never be proven one way or another. Comanche's background might have been one-quarter Mustang and three-quarters European or Spanish breeds. During the mid- to late nineteenth century, the army pursued interbreeding to produce a horse suited for the rugged western terrain. The idea at the time was to produce a hardier cavalry mount that might potentially match the fleeter, smaller tribal Mustangs.[8] Comanche may have been such a horse.

As was customary during that era, cavalry officers purchased their own mounts in private transactions, although at times, they also purchased government stock. Keogh, obviously taken with the horse, purchased Comanche from the remount pool at the relatively standard price of ninety dollars. In 2023 currency, that figure translates into a cost of $1,667. Officers often owned two horses—one horse was required for cross-country travel, and the other was kept fresh for battles or engagements. The officer's primary riding horse could easily become fatigued or "jaded" by the monotonous (and lengthy) overland travel. Lieutenant Keogh's long-distance horse was named Paddy—an "Eastern" horse described as a larger dark bay. History attests that Comanche's strength was reserved for combat.

What did he look like, and more specifically, what was his coat color? In a bit of a spoiler, Comanche is preserved for posterity in the Kansas University Museum of Natural History, where he appears to be a standard bay horse, meaning brown coat with black mane, tail, and legs. Remarkably, however, contemporary accounts list him as a sorrel, a "claybank," a claybank sorrel, a buckskin, dun-colored, or even a "dark, dirty sorrel."[9] Many accounts described him as a bit shaggy.

Keogh rode both Paddy and Comanche through 1870, when Paddy was reportedly sent back to Fort Riley due to fatigue. This meant that Comanche became Keogh's only mount. Again, the horse was wounded in June 1870, this time in the right leg, which kept him lame for several weeks. It is unknown which horse Keogh rode while Comanche recovered.

In one of the lesser-known facets of life after the Civil War, army units were often sent into the Reconstruction South to curb civil disturbances caused by the Ku Klux Klan and northern carpetbaggers. Keogh's career sent him south, where he and his company got into a fight with moonshiners on January 28, 1873. Comanche sustained yet another wound: this time in the right shoulder. The injury, that time, was apparently slight and he recovered quickly.

During the 1870s, the plains continued to experience flashpoints of discontent, broken promises, and ensuing hostilities with the tribes. The Dakota and Montana Territories were contested lands encompassing tribal hunting ranges. Keogh was assigned to Fort Abercrombie, but in the winter of 1873, he and Comanche wintered at Fort Totten in North Dakota. During that deployment, Comanche and Lieutenant Keogh covered nearly fifteen hundred miles, offering protection for the International Survey Commission that worked along the Canadian border.

In 1875, Troops I and D rejoined the 7th Cavalry at Fort Lincoln in the Dakota Territory. In 1876, the Battle of the Little Bighorn ended eight years of storied, and mutual, companionship between Keogh and Comanche. Although the outcome of the battle is well known, the specific details of what transpired to Custer's men in the heat of the battle is subject to a great amount of conjecture.

During the ensuing years, Comanche's fame grew as the "cult of Custer" grew. The gelding became the second commanding officer of the 7th Cavalry in Fort Riley, Kansas. He came to symbolize the glory and the tragedy surrounding the "lost" 7th Cavalry. When Keogh's horse took to the parade ground, heavy symbolism joined him. In a practice called the *lone charger*, the gelding was draped in black netting and a riderless saddle carried a pair of boots reversed in the stirrups. This symbolic image in the United States was first recorded for Alexander Hamilton's funeral in 1795. The practice most often symbolized a warrior who had fallen in battle (as was the case for Custer and his men, including Keogh), although the ceremony has been performed for US presidents on occasion.

Now instead of chasing across the wide-open plains, this ceremonial commemoration of the tragedy was Comanche's newest duty, and the army took it seriously.

Of course, the romance of the horse called to several of the wives and daughters at the post. The ladies wanted to take turns riding the heroic horse to the point of becoming a nuisance. In the end, Colonel Sturgis wrote the following, somewhat exasperated, order:

HEADQUARTERS

SEVENTH U.S. CAVALRY

FORT ABRAHAM LINCOLN, DAKOTA TERRITORY

General Orders No. 7

April 10, 1878.

1. The horse known as "Comanche," being the only living representative of the bloody tragedy of the Little Big Horn, Mont.,
   June 25, 1876, his kind treatment and comfort should be a matter of special pride and solicitude on the part of the 7th Cavalry,
   to the end that his life may be prolonged to the utmost limit.
   Though wounded and scarred, his very silence speaks in terms
   more eloquent than words of the desperate struggle against
   overwhelming numbers of the hopeless conflict, and heroic
   manner in which all went down that day.
2. The commanding officer of I Troop will see that a special and
   comfortable stall is fitted up for Comanche: he will not be ridden by any person whatever under any circumstances, nor will
   he be put to any kind of work.
3. Hereafter upon all occasions of ceremony (of mounted regimental formation), Comanche, saddled, bridled, draped in mourning, and led by a mounted trooper of Troop I, will be paraded
   with the regiment.

By Command of Colonel Sturgis
(Signed) E.A. Garlington,
1st Lieutenant and Adjutant,
7th U.S. Cavalry[10]

That put the squabbles of "who would ride Comanche next" to rest.

Comanche continued, although no longer ridden, to accompany
Troop I throughout Nebraska on scouting missions and skirmishes,
although he never entered battle again. Gustave Korn, a private who

served on one of the hilltop divisions of the Little Bighorn and is credited with nursing Comanche back to health, formed a very strong bond with Keogh's mount and vice versa.

Comanche, it must be admitted, became a bit of a character in his later years. He was allowed the freedom of the post and was the only living creature that wandered at will over the parade ground without reprimand. When the bugle sounded "formation," Comanche would trot out to his place in front of the line of Troop I.

An enduring favorite, he reportedly would be given sugar cubes upon demand in the officer's quarters and would "saunter" down to the enlisted men's canteen where a specially placed bucket of beer awaited him. In fact, it is claimed that Comanche grew fond of spirits. "It is not amiss to say that Comanche became an inveterate 'toper,'" according to Maj. Edwin S. Luce.[11]

One anecdotal story about Comanche's fondness for Gustave Korn recounts how, when the unit returned to Fort Riley, Korn paid a visit to a lady in a nearby town. When Private Korn did not return to base to feed and groom Comanche that evening as expected, the horse searched the base. Failing to locate Korn, it is claimed that Comanche tracked the private directly to the lady's house with the intent of escorting Korn back to the post.[12] Although it strikes a bit unlikely that a horse tracked a man to a stranger's house in another town . . . well, one never knows.

As fate played out, Gustav Korn took part in the Battle of Wounded Knee on December 29, 1890, during the Ghost Dance. He was killed. Comanche lost his second companion—his relationship with Korn lasted fourteen years. It is said that, although the 7th Cavalry returned to Fort Riley by train on January 26, 1891, Comanche lost interest in pretty much everything and his will gave out. On November 6, 1891, he died of colic. He was believed to be twenty-nine years old at the time.[13]

The official transcript provides the following:

Name	Comanche
Age	6 years at date of purchase; 25 years at date of transfer to Captain Nowlan
Height	15 hands

Weight	925 pounds
Color	Buckskin
Peculiar Markings	Left Hind fetlock, white-black tail, black mane—white marks on back—small white star on forehead—12 scars caused by wounds
Condition	Unserviceable
Date of Purchase	April 3, 1868
By Whom	space left blank
Cost	$90
Purchased at	St. Louis, Mo.
Remarks	Excused from all duties per General Order No. 7, Hdqrs. 7 US Cav, dated April 10, 1878. Ridden by Capt. Myles Keogh in Battle of the Little Big Horn River, M.T., June 25, 1876.

I certify that the preceding is a correct transcript from the records of Non-Commissioned staff and band, 7 Cav.

Station: Fort Meade, D.T   (signed)   JAMES D. THEMOR
Date: July 25, 87   2nd Lieutenant
                                         7 Cav
                                         Acting Adj.[14]

Instead of being buried, as was the case for most horses, Comanche was taxidermized. This additional practice provided some clarifications and yet another layer of mystery. Over time, conflicting and contradicting claims surfaced as to how severe and how many wounds the warrior sustained. Professor Lewis L. Dyche spent the summer of 1887 in Washington, DC, training under the auspices of the National Museum's chief taxidermist, William Temple Hornaday. In 1891, the US Army approached Dyche with the request that he preserve Comanche.[15] When Dyche performed Comanche's taxidermy, he located three severe wounds that occurred at the Little Bighorn: in his neck, lung, and groin. Four other wounds were considered flesh, or superficial.[16]

Over time, at one juncture Comanche was deemed improperly taken care of by the museum. In order to ensure his well being, a movement in 1947 came underway to return the famous horse to the army's custody and Fort Riley. This transfer was spearheaded by Edwin S. Luce. Ultimately, the University of Kansas and the museum retained Comanche, where he is now displayed prominently in a place of honor, and in fine repair.

He Nupa Wanika's Fabulous Blue Roan

Another horse that participated in the Battle of the Little Bighorn has become an icon in Lakota art. He is the mighty blue roan war horse of Hunkpapa Lakota known as No Two Horns (in Lakota *He Nupa Wanika*), the cousin of Sitting Bull. Born perhaps in 1852, No Two Horns became a well-known and prolific artist whose works are housed in museums all over the country. He is best known today for his paintings and "carved horse memorials." It is noted that it was a custom "that when a warrior had a horse killed under him in battle, he had the right to have this honorable memorial made and placed among his trophies."[17] All of his attributable carved horse memorials seem to depict the same horse reportedly killed in the Battle of the Little Bighorn when No Two Horns was likely twenty-four years of age. In later interviews, he referred to the horse as gray, but his artwork seems to consistently depict a large, blue horse. A blue roan, some people say.

One particular horse memorial attributed to He Nupa Wanika epitomizes the best of Plains Indian art. Arthur Amiotte, a contemporary Oglala Lakota artist, discussed the famous horse memorial or effigy which depicts a full-body horse wonderfully leaping forward through space and time:

> There was a gathering afterward at which time the warriors would get up and speak about their role in the battle and what they underwent, and to some degree, how their horses assisted them in surviving these great battles. They were referred to as "kill talks." . . . They talked about the event afterward and valorized their age mates—their fellow warriors—and themselves in terms of what they had done during the

battle, and also the role that the horse played in the success of the event. . . . But the way this horse's carver does that is different . . . It's the personification, almost a monumentalizing of the horse, like many equestrian pieces—the whole way the horse is configured speaks to us of the actions of the horse and the owner during the encounter. And this particular piece captures the movement.[18]

Regardless of whether Two No Horns is the creative force behind the effigy, he proved a prolific and talented artist. In fact, according to the State Historical Society of North Dakota that homes a large collection of He Nupa Wanika's work, fully half of them contain horses.

He plainly carried the loss of that "blue roan" horse with him all his remaining days.

VIC AND DANDY

Custer, the Lieutenant Colonel who led the disastrous Battle of the Little Bighorn, is often portrayed as an avid horseman, with a few serious reservations. He might have been daring, dashing, and a fearless rider, but that didn't mean he was a true "horseman." At the time of the Little Bighorn, Custer had two mounts in his possession, which he brought along to the field. They were named Vic and Dandy. On the day of the battle, no one knows why, he changed from his favorite horse Dandy to Vic, who he had obtained three years earlier. According to Custer's orderly, Pvt. John Burkman, Custer and he had discussed the possibility of retiring Dandy after that current campaign concluded.

"Dandy's age is beginning to tell on him a little,"[19] Custer claimed.

That being said, Dandy was eleven years old and Vic twelve—neither horse too old for battle. Dandy was acquired from army consignments and was known throughout the 7th for his "dancing" and fiery temperament. Vic (whose real name was Victory) was a Kentucky Thoroughbred with a reputation for being fast. True, Dandy had been ridden the previous day, and Custer might have considered him "spent." There is also that lingering account, corroborated by officers the night before the battle, that Custer acted unnaturally subdued and out of character. Did he have a premonition of his fate? If so, that might have been a contributing reason why he decided to spare his favorite horse.

Vic was the mount that Custer rode into battle.

Stepping backward in time, Custer had been a Brevet General in the Civil War. Like many other officers, once the war ended his rank diminished, as experienced by most other regular army officers. Custer wanted to be called "General," although his rank no longer supported that position. Nevertheless, he was anxious to make his name in the West. The first horse he bought after the Civil War was a five-year-old bay jumper and gelding named King Bernadotte. The asking price was four hundred dollars, which translates into about $9,500 dollars in recent exchange. Then Custer heard about another horse—Victory: a foal born in 1864 of superior Kentucky breeding.

In 1871, the 7th was assigned to Elizabethtown, Kentucky, to suppress Ku Klux Klan activities and to break up private liquor stills. Custer, charged with procuring horses for the regiment and already a lover of horses, began to think of himself, and fashion himself, as an owner and breeder of fine racehorses.

In Elizabethtown, Custer acquired a confiscated stallion named Don Juan.

Some sources claim the stallion was unrideable. Whatever the case, Custer lost control of him at the Washington Grand Review of the Armies—he "bolted past President Andrew Johnson, Ulysses S. Grant, and other dignitaries in the reviewing stand. Custer, in the melee, lost his hat and saber and made headlines, though not particularly favorable ones."[20] The entire event caused many Custer skeptics to question whether the mad dash was the result of poor horse handling ability or whether the performance came down to typical Custer bravado and attention seeking.

Perhaps as a direct result of the unfavorable coverage, Custer shipped the stallion to Michigan and put him out to stud. Unfortunately, the horse proved to have a short career in that aspect as well. Just one year later, Don Juan died from a burst blood vessel. No doubt Custer lost a fair amount of money on that investment beyond suffering a blot on his reputation.

Once Custer acquired Vic in 1872, he had him immediately gelded.

The man had a tough record with horses, which, even contemporaneously, resulted in criticisms.

During his Civil War career, Custer reportedly had eleven horses shot out from underneath him. Not to mention that in 1867, he shot and killed his own horse while hunting buffalo. Poor King Bernadotte would suffer a similar fate on August 11, 1873, during a western skirmish with the Sioux.

In 1876, Custer rode Vic into the Battle of the Little Bighorn after splitting his regiment of nearly seven hundred men (including scouts and civilians) into four parts, and those parts divided into further companies. One company stayed behind to take care of the supplies and the civilians. Three companies each were assigned to Reno and three to Benteen. Custer retained five companies consisting of about 225 officers and troops. Although Custer's command was annihilated, there were some of his men who were stragglers or who never reached the battlefield for one reason or another. Those men who survived provided much of the information available today, although no one knows precisely what happened on the field of battle during the demise of Custer's command.

It is part of the mystery that Custer's horse Vic was never positively identified among the dead.

Custer's defeat was an unmitigated failure in the young country's history. Because it was such a blow as to how the "Boy General" could have suffered such an ignominious defeat, a cult of Custer was born. And part of that cult was the desperation to learn whether Vic had indeed died alongside his master or whether he had survived. The accounts are conflicting.

There is only one known and verified picture of Vic, and only three of his white socks are visible. The first question posed is whether Vic had three white socks or four. Again, the responses differ. Many of Reno and Benteen's men walked the field after the battle, pressed into burial details in the immediate and horrific aftermath. There are many references to the gruesome remainders, the bodies (both man and equine) bloated and rotting in the heat; the stench was described as unbearable. Through the tangle of corpses, men searched for Custer and Vic.

Some of the men who knew Vic claimed that he survived, while others who likewise knew Vic claimed that he had died. When speaking, in later years, to Lakota or Cheyenne warriors who had taken part in the battle, many of them claimed Vic survived. A Miniconjou Lakota named Iron Hail (and later known as Dewey Beard) told his adopted son in the 1930s that Vic had survived and was taken by a Santee warrior named Walks-Under-the-Ground. Sitting Bull himself believed a fine sorrel that was taken with them up to Canada in November 1876 was indeed Custer's horse. Vic, or perhaps another horse, may have been sold to a Canadian officer as a possibility recounted in Elizabeth Atwood's book *His Very Silence Speaks*. Not attributing the identity to Vic, she describes a gray horse bearing the 7th Cavalry brand and purchased by Canadian Superintendent James M. Walsh of the Northwest Mounted Police.

Presumed to have been captured during the Custer battle, the horse was brought to Canada with the American Indians who had fled

George Armstrong Custer's horses in his possession at the time of the Little Big-horn. Dandy is on the left and is the darker of the two horses. Vic, who accompanied Custer into battle, is on the right.
LIBRARY OF CONGRESS.

northward after their victory. Walsh wrote to General Terry, offering to return the horse to the 7th Cavalry. "But," he added, "of the many relics I have seen of the battle of the Little Big Horn, none have taken my fancy like this old trooper."[21]

Superintendent Walsh received permission to keep the horse, who he named "Custer." None other than Sitting Bull remembered the horse, reportedly pleased that his friend possessed the mount.

Superintendent Walsh, also referred to as Major Walsh, kept the horse for many years and provided him with the best of care, "until he passed along."[22]

But back to Vic and Dandy. If Vic survived and made his way to Canada, he did not capture attention, nor was he identified. Regardless, Vic certainly had an eventful life . . . and hopefully a long one.

Dandy, Custer's favorite horse, was left that fateful day with the pack train and survived, although he was slightly wounded even at four miles southwest of Custer's hill. The wound was not serious, and he was shipped back to Michigan to Custer's widow, Libby, who gave the horse to Custer's elderly father. It is said that Dandy reflected his rider. Although he had been a firebrand for Custer, when his elderly father was seated upon him, Dandy behaved accordingly. It is said that whenever Buffalo Bill and the Wild West show stopped in the vicinity, Cody would drop by to pay his respects to Custer's father and the horse.

Dandy died at twenty-four years of age and is buried in Custer's only surviving brother—Nevin's—orchard.

A historical plaque stands in Monroe, Michigan, commemorating the Custer House. Dandy, his steadfast horse, is memorialized on that plaque, which states that he remains buried in the orchard.

Western Horse Trivia

Horses captured in skirmishes were considered spoils of war and were led away as both mementos and as booty.

NOTES

1. Elizabeth Atwood Lawrence, *His Very Silence Speaks: Comanche—The Horse Who Survived Custer's Last Stand*, Detroit, Wayne State University Press, 1989, 74.

2. John G. Bourke, *On the Border with Crook*, New York, NY: Charles Scribner's Sons, 1891, 371.

3. Edward Smith Luce, *Keogh, Comanche and Custer*, Buffalo Grove, IL: John S. Swift Co. Inc., 1939, 65.

4. Luce, *Keogh, Comanche and Custer*, 66.

5. Lawrence, *His Very Silence Speaks*, 36.

6. Luce, *Keogh, Comanche and Custer*, 8.

7. National Park Service, "Washita Battlefield: Lt. Col. Alfred H. Sully (1821–1879)," https://www.nps.gov/waba/learn/historyculture/lt-col-alfred-h-sully-1821-1879.htm#:~:text=In%20September%20of%201868%2C%20with,during%20the%20summer%20of%201868.

8. Lawrence, *His Very Silence Speaks*, 40.

9. Lawrence, *His Very Silence Speaks*, 45.

10. Lawrence, *His Very Silence Speaks*, 105.

11. Luce, *Keogh, Comanche and Custer*, 68.

12. Luce, *Keogh, Comanche and Custer*, 69.

13. Anthony A. Amaral, *Comanche: The Horse that Survived the Custer Massacre*, Los Angeles, Westernlore Press, 1961, 42.

14. Amaral, *Comanche*, 50.

15. G. Joseph Pierron, "Lewis Lindsey Dyche," Kansas State Historical Society, https://www.kshs.org/kansapedia/lewis-lindsay-dyche/18149.

16. Amaral, *Comanche*, 80.

17. David L. Wooley and Joseph D. Horse Capture, "Joseph No Two Horns: He Nupe Wanica," *American Indian Art Magazine* (Summer 1993), 34, http://faculty.washington.edu/kbunn/Wooley.pdf.

18. Lance Nixon, "Bounding Home: Masterpiece of Plains Indian Sculpture returns to South Dakota," October 8, 2015, *Capital Journal*, https://www.capjournal.com/news/bounding-home-masterpiece-of-plains-indian-sculpture-returns-to-south-dakota/article_85933c9a-6e38-11e5-828e-1f6bf2faad8b.html.

19. Sharon B. Smith, "Vic at the Little Big Horn," *Wild West Magazine*, June 2022, 34.

20. Smith, "Vic at the Little Big Horn," 36.

21. Lawrence, *His Very Silence Speaks*, 29.

22. Lawrence, *His Very Silence Speaks*, 30.

CHAPTER 8

HORSE THIEVES AND THE LARCENY OF LIVESTOCK

Always a touchy subject, horse thieves were literally the scourge of the West. In today's culture, the reasoning behind their despised status is somewhat different than one might suspect. While the theft of a horse throughout history has always meant the loss of a precious companion, in yesteryear, the reasons *why* horse theft was considered a serious crime had to do with distances and the prevailing opinions toward prisons and their occupants.

Vigilante justice played into law and order on the range. Location played into the rationale.

If a horse located in a city or town setting was stolen, obviously the theft resulted in a financial loss. Beyond the upsetting emotions and financial implications, the larceny of a city horse signaled a detriment to a person's ability to earn a living, much less travel. Horses were indispensable for doctors' house calls at a distance, haulers' basic means of a livelihood, merchants' deliveries, and livery proprietors' reputation and rental businesses, to name just a few horse-dependent occupations. City horse theft proved a nuisance, but seldom a danger. Farmers would find themselves unable to plough, mow hay, and those types of necessary tasks.

But it was the open range where matters turned deadly.

Should a horse be stolen on the range or in the wild, the consequences could turn life-threatening on a dime.

Take the hypothetical example of someone riding out in the vicinity of Chugwater, Wyoming, in the middle of the wide-open empty.

Ranchland may have been claimed in that area, but whether someone owned the land or whether it was true "open range" made little difference in the isolation. Isolation, in those days, often meant the complete absence of help should the need arise. Ranch headquarters and houses could easily prove few and far between. A person left horseless in remote swaths of the West found themselves at a distinct disadvantage. The chances of rescue or assistance by chance were next to non-existent.

So, if a cowboy loped along on a particularly fine mount, and his path crossed that of an outlaw who had an eye for his fine horse, the outlaw might aim his gun, cock the hammer, and threaten, "Your life or your horse." Perhaps the cowboy dismounted and watched the outlaw ride off, taking his horse along for company. Or he fought and took a bullet in the struggle to maintain control of the horse. Both outcomes could prove deadly.

Now horseless, the cowboy finds he has no better choice than to start walking. But walk where and in which direction? Fort Laramie is thirty-five miles away as the crow flies, but does the cowboy even have his bearings to the point where he knows that critical piece of information? Depending upon the season, he could easily freeze to death in the winter. In the hot summer sun, yes, the distance is walkable in two days or so. But he surely might die of thirst if he does not encounter drinkable water along the way.

Should the now-horseless man turn out fortunate enough to find a fence, he could stay along the fence line. If he found a stream, perhaps by following the water downriver, he would find a settlement—this was not guaranteed, but at least it offered a measure of hope.

Then again, that life-preserving stream might simply dry out in the middle of nothing and nowhere.

The chance of misadventure or death remained high riding alone on the range, but for a person on foot, left alone in the vast space without a horse, it significantly increased.

It is claimed that more men were hung for stealing horses in the Old West than they ever were for murder.

Horse thieves operated alone or in gangs and associations. They existed in every western state or territory. Newspapers often carried their exploits as a matter of public service, and a warning to stay alert:

> Pursuit of Horse Thieves. Denver, April 4.—A Cheyenne special says: All the northern sheriffs are at full cry on the trail of a desperate gang of wholesale horse thieves. The freebooters, finding themselves closely pursued, cut the telegraph wires. This left Johnson, Sheridan, Big Horn and northern Carbon counties entirely out of it. The thieves have, by this time, reached Montana with 200 head of Wyoming horses.[1]

The loss of two hundred head of horses was never a small matter.

Vigilantes took such crimes seriously . . . and into their own hands.

Whether the law approved or not (and it usually didn't), a notable lack of indignation was found in the newspapers where the killings of presumed horse thieves were concerned. Part of the tolerance for vigilantism stemmed from the scarcity of a basic commodity: food out on the frontier. All foods had to be grown, slaughtered, prepared, or otherwise shipped in. In accordance with sentiments of the time, law-abiding citizens didn't necessarily approve of *feeding* someone who "sat" in prison. Due to that very fundamental concern, criminals in the 1860s until around the turn of the last century served much shorter sentences than one might expect. Their sentences were certainly more lenient timewise than today . . . even for serious crimes such as murder.

And remember, murder and horse theft were viewed as equivalent.

As for the gang of thieves heading to Montana with Wyoming horses, they posed a very real problem to society at that time.

Vigilantes organized themselves to combat crime in what they viewed as the absence or leniency of law enforcement. Reportedly, one organization in Colorado was called the Uplift Society because of its motto: "It is essential to forgive all horse thieves, and they can best be forgiven after they are hanged."[2]

The Outlaws

Stealing horses came down to different reasons, as varied as the backgrounds of accused horse thieves themselves.

Whether the thieves worked alone, in bands, or even in networks, they were considered a scourge throughout the West.

One of the first horse thieves in Colorado's early territorial days (then considered a part of Kansas Territory) was suspended from a cottonwood tree in 1860. The capture of a white man called "Black Hawk" elicited the confession that "he was a member of a great organization of horse-thieves operating through the country all the way across from southern Wisconsin." Before he was hanged, he implicated the ringleaders—Denver attorney A.C. Ford and John Shear, both politically powerful men in the Colorado Territory. John Shear acted as a Denver City Council member and was described at the time as "big, fat and rather dissipated." He was also a founder of Denver's first library.[3]

These two were not the type of men "normally" considered to be horse thieves or implicated in a ring of such activities. But in the early days, horse stealing provided a tempting and profitable business.

DENVER CITY, Thursday, Sept. 6, 1860.

The night before last JOHN SHEAR, who formerly resided at Newaygo, Michigan, where he has a wife and family, and who kept the Vasquez Hotel in Auraria or West Denver, during last Fall and Winter, was secretly hanged to a tree a mile above Denver, on the Platte, for having been found to be a prominent member of a party of horse-stealers which has been infesting this section. SHEAR was found in the morning hanging from a tree, above town, with a piece of paper pinned to his clothes, on which was written, "This man John Shear was hung by us citizens. It was proven that he is a horse thief." The knot was tied in regular hangman's style, and the performance seemed to have been executed by experienced hands. . . .

SHEAR was reported to be one of the principal men in the gang, which fact was confirmed to be an absolute certainty by evidence. The remains of SHEAR were taken from where they were hung to the City

Hospital here, where they were properly coffined, and removed to the burying-ground and decently interred.

All manner of reports and rumors of hangings have been rife on the streets here during the past thirty hours, and it is believed that six or seven more men have been found swinging from limbs of trees up and down the Platte and on Cherry Creek, above town. Some firms are said to have sent on their orders for heavy supplies of hemp rope . . .

A.C. FORD, Esq., . . . a lawyer of considerable ability was suspected, and, as we hear, proven to be president of a party of evil doers here. He left in the express coach yesterday morning for Leavenworth city to defend that desperado, JAMES A. GORDON, at Leavenworth. He was followed down the road four or five miles by six or eight citizens of this region, mounted on horseback, with loaded rifles, who stopped the coach, in which were five or six passengers for the States, and ordered FORD to step out. . . . FORD, seeing the six or eight men with leveled rifles, left the vehicle, and accompanied his captors over a few miles on Eight Mile Creek, where he was shot or strung up for his reputed deeds. Exceptions have been taken to-day by some of our citizens to the summary action, and a meeting is called in front of the post-office, on Larimer-street, to "organize an effective plan of punishing offenders against the public good, and to prevent further cases of 'hanging after night,' and on the spur of the moment."[4]

There are a couple of background points that are important to consider when reading such accounts. Newspapers in the nineteenth century, and indeed into the twentieth century, served a couple of different purposes. True, they delivered the news, but that news could have a slant. They were also an early form of entertainment. Between the years 1860 and 1865 alone, the publishers Beadle and Adams published more than five million dime novels.[5] Newspapermen would be keen to notice the competition and would try to capitalize on winning reader share. The age of the dime novels ran through 1915. All of this adds to the entertainment angle of the stories published in newspapers of the time.

The story out of Denver's lynching in 1860 sticks to the facts in the main but tries to fill in the reader as to "who" these thieves were, where they came from, and their individual backgrounds.

The Musgrove gang of horse thieves and cattle rustlers operated out of a northern Colorado hideout in an abandoned stage station called Bonner Springs. From there the gang operated throughout southern Wyoming and northern Colorado, stealing horses, mules, and cattle. Their favorite targets were government animals. Of course, in that day and age, Cheyenne, Sioux, and other tribes were often falsely accused of the thefts, providing cover for Musgrove and his men. In the dark of night in September 1864, a herd of fifty head of cattle were stolen from Fort Steele in Wyoming. The next month, it is claimed that *all* of the cavalry horses were taken . . . a claim which will strike the modern reader as suspicious.

Keep in mind that cavalry horses were always branded, so could therefore be identified as belonging to the US government.

Nevertheless, the gang operated up and down the Front Range, following the Cherokee and Overland Trails. City Marshal Dave Cook of Denver tracked Musgrove down in Golden, Colorado, in November 1868. He escorted his prisoner to Denver, where vigilantes stole the horse-thief ringleader from jail and strung him up until dead. According to newspaper accounts, the jailers did little to nothing to resist. Largely, it appears, because of Musgrove's bragging that his "friends" would rescue him.[6]

As time progressed and lynching became less common, it didn't completely die out. A lot of the "law" or lack of legalities depended upon the location.

One of the most famous of all western horse thieves was a man called "Dutch Henry" Born. Much was made of Dutch Henry in his time, as he was reputedly the head man of a large ring of horse thieves that some estimated as numbering three hundred strong. It is claimed Dutch Henry's ring of thieves operated throughout the western states of Texas, Oklahoma, Kansas, Colorado, and New Mexico.

Dutch Henry garnered plenty of newspaper space when he was arrested in Trinidad, Colorado, in 1879. According to accounts of the incident, Henry was characterized as "the Leading Horse Thief of the West." In the region's lore, it is claimed that Dutch Henry commanded a syndicate of three hundred horse thieves in various states, towns, and territories.

On one of Henry's forays, he was tracked into Colorado by Deputy US Marshal Charles B. Jones of Wichita. The lawman cabled Marshal Wilcox of Pueblo, and together they went to arrest their man in the town of Trinidad. They had caught wind that Henry was in the Commercial Hotel. When the law officers approached the hotel's landlord, he affirmed that a man matching their description was registered. In the colorful prose of the nineteenth century (additional details provided for entertainment value), the following excerpt of the full printed account ran:

> The landlord led the way up a winding stair, lighting the course of his footsteps with a tallow candle. He proceeded to a small room on the third story and opened the door according to instructions, without knocking. The occupant of the only bed turned on his pillow as the light struck him when the officers were convinced that he was their man. . . .

> "Hold up your hands, Henry."

> . . . The true history of Dutch Henry's life would make a volume . . . of wild daring and hair-breadth escapes. . . . He is of medium height and size, and pithy, agile and muscular. His complexion is brown and his eyes inclined to be blue. His features are intelligent and he is said to be possessed of a good education. He positively refuses to tell the secret of his life, but it is considered certain that there is some mystery connected with his career which has perhaps forced him to adopt the life he now leads. . . . Henry is the leader of a powerful band of horse thieves who operate throughout the western country. . . . They devote themselves to horses and mules as a general thing, and often drive away entire herds from the places where they are grazing or from their stables. They have been known to attack various herds of government stock when the soldiers were in sight, and as for the Indians, they consider themselves privileged to take their stock whenever the least occasion offers. Henry . . . carries twenty-four bullet marks as proof of

the character of the life he has led. He has been shot and cut from top to toe, from Dakota to Texas.[7]

Tongue and cheek accounts aside, Dutch Henry was reported in Colorado again during June of 1880. It seems that somehow Henry must have escaped his confines and returned into the Roaring Fork Valley of Colorado. Again, wry newspaper coverage followed, this account adding:

> Nothing was seen of him in that section until the Cheyenne raid, when he followed the government troops, picking up horses. The people gathered together and attempted to capture him, but in spite of their efforts, he got off with a herd which he subsequently sold in Kansas and Missouri, branding a C over the government brand and forging bills of sale. If he gets clear of Colorado this time he will probably go to Utah, as he seems to be obeying the injunction to go west.[8]

Dutch Henry's career turned out to be so prolific that the term *Dutch Henrys* came to mean stolen horses.

This article does point out two prevailing opinions of the time. The theft of "Indian horses" did not matter, and the theft of government stock didn't seem to be taken all that seriously either, except by the government itself, and the law officials. The average citizen seemed not to care. This is a theme that repeats itself over and over.

THE "GOLDEN-TOOTHED LOVER OF OTHER FOLKS' CATTLE AND HORSEFLESH"

James Middleton Riley was born in 1851 in Texas. In 1872, the prosecutor in Coryell County, Texas, indicted him for stealing a mare. Two years later, Riley stole a gelding worth seventy-five dollars and landed himself on the Texas Rangers' fugitive list in 1874. Not wanting to deal with looking over his shoulder for the Rangers, he hastened north to North Platte, Nebraska. By the time he reached Nebraska, some claimed that he already had four or five names, and that he was called "Doc" because of his ability to "doctor" brands.[9]

In Nebraska, he found work with the Powers Cattle Company. Some sources claim he was a good cowhand; others claim he was, at best, indifferent. One thing for certain was the "honest" or "straight life" did not suit him, and in 1877 he was arrested near Julesburg, Colorado, for stealing thirty-four horses.

Apparently, the cell in which he was held had a dirt floor, and he dug his way to freedom. His fame soared as a result.[10]

In the spring of 1877, Middleton and his gang, known as the Pony boys, focused their efforts in the Niobrara River valley. However, his fame had spread so wide that reports of his gang's activity spread throughout the state. Some even believed that Middleton controlled a state-wide criminal organization, but as author Harold Hutton states, "How such organization and discipline could be possible among as large a number of lawless and undisciplined men as were engaged in stock stealing baffles[s] the imagination."[11]

Middleton was a smart man. He contented himself with stealing horses from the Lakotas and Cheyenne. The remainder of the thieving was left to his associates. Chief Little Wound of the Pine Ridge agency complained that Middleton stole 590 head of their horses. By his own community, he was however lauded as a type of Robin Hood figure. The settlers in the region figured the Lakotas stole their horses, and Doc Middleton was just retrieving their stolen property. In a two-year period, it is claimed that Doc Middleton stole two thousand to three thousand head of horses. The arrangements ran Nebraska horses down to Kansas for cheap sale. Middleton would then steal Kansas horses and turn right around and drive them north to Nebraska for cheap sale once again.[12]

Eventually, the law caught up with him. Using a ruse, a lawman named Llewellyn said he had a pardon to offer, but instead shot Middleton in the stomach and hauled him back to Cheyenne, Wyoming, for trial. Doc ended up in the penitentiary, but when released, he cleaned up his life and became a saloon owner in Orin Junction, Wyoming. After a knife fight broke out behind his bar, Middleton was arrested not for the fight, but for the fact that he didn't hold a liquor license. He was sentenced to jail where he contacted erysipelas, a severe skin disease, which turned into pneumonia.

Doc Middleton died on December 27, 1913, and is buried in Douglas, Wyoming. Some outlaws like Butch Cassidy expanded upon Doc's basic horse theft and created an extortion system in Wyoming. Eventually, he was sent to prison for stealing a five-dollar horse. Does that sound a bit odd? Of course it does. Chances were that the law found the five-dollar horse an easy charge to press instead of the far more serious operation. Strangely enough, Cassidy's "neighbors" in the vicinity supported his early release from prison. The reason for that apparent forgiveness points to the likelihood that those involved and within Cassidy's reach upon release desired to stay on Cassidy's good side.

They wanted to avoid acts of retaliation.

As a matter of record, Butch Cassidy served between July 12, 1894, and January 20, 1896. That's eighteen months of a two-year prison term.

FEMALE HORSE THIEVES

Women, from the scant records available, tended to act the part of fences for stolen horses, rather than committing the actual theft themselves. The notable exception to this rule came in the form of Flora Mundis, aka Tom King of Oklahoma. Tall tales abound concerning Flora Quick/Mundis/ China Dot and presumably back to Flora, this time in the company of a

A staged reenactment of a horse thief hanging, 1898
T. W. INGERSOLL.

A real posse with their horses in Tipton, Wyoming. Butch Cassidy was the train robber.
WYOMING STATE ARCHIVES.

man named Bill Garland. This crossdressing woman was better known in horse-thieving circles by the name Tom King.

It is difficult to determine where the truth ends and the story making starts with this flamboyant character. This four foot, eight inch, 130 pound lady may have originated from the area near Guthrie, Oklahoma. Again, her past is murky because there is a credible newspaper article on her family history claiming she was from Holden, Missouri.[13] According to the Plains Indian & Pioneers Museum, this "plains pirate" was the daughter of a wealthy farmer who died when she was fifteen. Left an estate of twenty-three hundred acres and thirteen thousand dollars in cash, it was a sizable inheritance for the time. Flora married a man named Ora Mundis, who was only after her money. A tired story, but true: When the money ran out, so did he. It is believed that Flora turned to prostitution, then began dressing in men's clothing to steal horses and changed her name to Tom King.[14]

Beyond committing acts of horse theft, she hung out with a "rough crowd" and proved talented at jailbreaks:

MISS "TOM KING"

The Story of the Escape of This Beautiful but Notorious Thief

The escape of the notorious female horse thief, known in the territory as "Tom King," from the county jail turns out to be one of the romances of the new country. "Tom" is a very handsome and fascinating young lady of about 22 years, with a voice like a dove and an eye that knows no deceit. She is a quarter blood Cherokee Indian, and many of her relatives and people live near Springfield, Mo., whence her ancestors emigrated to the Cherokee country. Her operations in the territory have been extensive and notorious, and her captures frequent, but she is never brought to trial . . . a year ago she was arrested . . . [and] held in the Guthrie jail . . . [and] unaccountably escaped. A while later she was held in the Oklahoma City jail, and thence escaped in the same inexplicable way. For the last three months she has been in the new jail of Canadian county. Last night she walked out the open doors of the jail dressed in her ordinary female habiliments, but under which she had taken the precaution to wear her full suit of men's clothing, which the courtesy of the officers allowed her to keep. Outside of the door the skirts disappeared, and a very good looking, youthful man apparently bestrode a convenient horse and rode safely out of the city. . . . The undersheriff of the county has not been seen since a few minutes before the escape, and two of his five horses are not to be found. . . . The grand jury investigated the case of the escape. . . . It is known that the disappearing officer was much taken with the comely woman.—Cor. *St. Louis Globe-Democrat.*[15]

Apparently, Flora/Tom King's crime spree did not abate. While she was skilled in jail escapes, apparently, she didn't prove as adept at eluding capture in the first place. Another thing to note about newspapers of the time: Sometimes they "got it wrong," and a story circulated that was not true:

WAS A MISTAKE.

The Notorious Female Horsethief Not Captured at Fredonia. Kan. EL RENO, Ok., Aug. 12.—The recent report sent from Fredonia, Kan., that Mrs. Mundis, alias "Tom King" the notorious female horse-thief and bandit who broke jail here December 1 last and has since [been] at large, had been apprehended in that city proves to have been a mistake. The sheriff of this county has returned from there without the prisoner. A woman who answers the description of "Tom King" had been arrested by the sheriff of Wilson county, but was released before the Oklahoma sheriff arrived.[16]

This last article is worthy of inclusion in a dime novel. Edited for brevity, it is worth reading the entire account if interested:

A FRONTIER INCIDENT.

The Outcome of a Poker Game Among Bad Men. How a Noted Female Horsethief Demonstrated Her Proficiency In Her Special Line of Business—A Very Hard Crowd.

A queer crowd sat in a barroom at Caddo in Indian territory, a few months ago. They had drifted together in a dingy little barroom, one half of which was set apart for gambling. A rough gang had been gathering all evening, says the Chicago Times.... "Let's make it a jack pot," roared a big, red-faced man. with a terrific scar across his face and an evil eye in his head. . . . "Are you in, pard?" asked a third player, with only one eye, of the fourth party, evidently a stranger to the other three players. The latter was small, dudish, with a queer expression about the eyes and a peculiar shaped mouth. "Bet your life I'm with you," said the latter, as he planked in a big handful of silver. . . . Chips ran out and money took their place. The crowd gathered at the table and a fortune was soon in sight, "My money is all gone," finally ejaculated the dudish fellow with the queer eye. "I've got two good horses outside. 'I'll stake 'em. if you trot 'em in," said the others, with a knowing grin of delight. "The crowd'll see that you get a square deal, stranger." "The crowd be d—d," smiled the dapper youth. "I'll see to that myself." He went to the door and whistled, and soon two splendid ponies trotted up and were led in standing quietly by the table, while their master again sat and called the other players' hands.... "Four sixes ain't in it with four queens." growled the one-eyed man. He snarled like a wolf over a big meal as he tucked that bundle of money out of sight. and, rising, took the ponies outside and tied them. Then he returned and lined up to the bar with: "Everybody liquor." All responded except the dudish stranger, and he moved toward the door. No one noticed him glide out and he drew a bee line for his lost pony, mounted and raced away with a loud clatter. Mr. One-Eye dashed down his liquor and darted to the doorway—a string of oaths upon his lips, and began blazing away. A ringing laugh floated back, and a shrill voice exclaimed: "You've got my money . . . but you don't get Tom King's horse . . ." The outlaws returned to the bar and with many bitter oaths, drank to the health of "brave Tom King."[17]

Flora Quirk Mundis' life, unremarkably, did not have a happy ending. After marrying a Chinese immigrant and changing her name to China Dot, she became connected with a man named Bill Garland. According to the Plains Indian & Pioneer Museum, in 1903, the two "were high on opium and began quarreling. Garland shot Flora four times before turning the gun on himself."[18]

Belle Starr remains the West's most notorious woman associated with horse stealing. She had a fine eye for horses, by all accounts. The exact details of her life are murky with facts replaced by legend. While Belle was arrested for horse theft, it is probable that she acted as a fence, rather than performing the actual theft. Her death is also shrouded in mystery, although it is certain that she was murdered, the case has remained unsolved.

Western Horse Trivia

The last man rounded up by a posse for horse theft may have been in 1996 in Texas. The theft took place near Bosqueville, west of Waco.

NOTES

1. *Aspen Weekly Times*, April 5, 1890.
2. Gary Cartwright, "The Last Posse," March 1988, https://www.texasmonthly.com/articles/the-last-posse.

3. Stephen J. Leonard, *Lynching in Colorado 1859–1919*, Louisville,CO: University Press of Colorado, 2002, 22.

4. *New York Times*, "From Pike's Peak.; Lynch Law Triumphant Men Hung Without the Form of Trial," https://www.nytimes.com/1860/09/20/archives/from-pikes-peak -lynch-law-triumphant-men-hung-without-the-form-of.html.

5. Ann Marie Pope, "American Dime Novels 1860–1915," https://www.history .org.uk/student/resource/4512/american-dime-novels-1860-1915#:~:text =Between%201860%20and%201865%20alone,often%20came%20with%20camp%20life.

6. Leonard, *Lynching in Colorado*, 37–39.

7. *Colorado Daily Chieftain*, volume 8, number 2102, March 2, 1879, https:// www.coloradohistoricnewspapers.org/?a=d&d=CFT18790302-01.2 .21&srpos=1&e=-------en-20--1-byDA-img-txIN%7ctxCO%7ctxTA -%22Dutch+Henry%22+%22Horse+Thief%22-------0------.

8. *Leadville Weekly Herald*, June 12, 1880, https://www.coloradohistoricnewspapers .org/?a=d&d=LWH18800612.2.20&srpos=3&e=-------en-20--1-byDA-img -txIN%7ctxCO%7ctxTA-%22Dutch+Henry%22+%22Horse+Thief%22-------0------.

9. Nebraska Public Media, "Doc Middleton, the Unwickedest Outlaw," February 16, 2017, https://nebraskapublicmedia.org/en/series-media/nebraska-stories-video/season-8 -video-15886/doc-middleton-the-unwickedest-outlaw-50002086.

10. Matthew Luckett, *Never Caught Twice: Horse Stealing in Western Nebraska, 1850–1890*, Lincoln, NB: University of Nebraska Press, 2020, 146.

11. Luckett, *Never Caught Twice*, 146.

12. Nebraska Public Media, "Doc Middleton."

13. *Evansville Journal*, "'Tom King' A Woman. History of a Girl Who Became A Noted Horse Thief," Friday, August 18, 1893, Evansville, IN, 3.

14. Plains Indians & Pioneers Museum, Woodward, OK, https://www.facebook.com/ PIPMWoodward/photos/a.10150836469563717/10159488369033717/?type=3&source =57&locale=ms_MY&paipv=0&eav=AfYMJx88gGEB9YNMpuxYiaHDajHqC3IXna RSizSDdtC6OZzHlFQcsaxuELHvifDY96g&_rdr.

15. *Colorado Daily Chieftain*, January 26, 1894, Quoting *St. Louis Globe Democrat*, https://www.coloradohistoricnewspapers.org/?a=d&d=CFT18940126-01 .2.50&srpos=7&e=-------en-20--1-byDA-img-txIN%7ctxCO%7ctxTA -%22Tom+King%22+horse+thief-------0------.

16. *Rocky Mountain News (Daily)*, Volume 35, No. 225, August 13, 1894, https://www .coloradohistoricnewspapers.org/?a=d&d=RMD18940813-01.2.49&srpos=2&e=------ -en-20--1-img-txIN%7ctxCO%7ctxTA-%22Tom+King%22-------0------.

17. *Daily Sentinel (Grand Junction)*, Volume 1, No. 238, August 30, 1894, https:// www.coloradohistoricnewspapers.org/?a=d&d=DSL18940830-01.2.18&srpos=11&e= -------en-20--1-byDA-img-txIN%7ctxCO%7ctxTA-%22Tom+King%22+horse+thief -------0------.

18. Plains Indians & Pioneers Museum.

CHAPTER 9

MONTANA'S HORSE THIEF WAR, THE LAW, AND
THE ANTI-HORSE THIEF ASSOCIATIONS

The Deadwood Stage, Deadwood, South Dakota.
LIBRARY OF CONGRESS. JOHN C. H. GRABILL PHOTOGRAPHER.

HORSE THEFT REMAINED A PROBLEM THROUGHOUT THE WEST, BUT IN Montana, it flared to an outright war. Called the Horse Thief War, the flames fanned after the 1883 fall cattle roundups took place and the stock tallies were taken and compared. While the cattle losses experienced over the previous six months were alarming, the most shocking aspect of that tally was not the number of cattle that had been pilfered, but rather the number of horses. Horses traveled fast and could be rapidly moved out of the country or territory with comparative ease. Large Montana stock producer Con Kohrs favored a plan to send out a regiment of cowboys— similar to the idea supported by Teddy Roosevelt and the Marquis de Mores of the Dakota Territory—to deal with the raiders. Roosevelt and de Mores wanted to form an "army of cowboys" to string up every horse thief encountered. At that time there were few, if any, stockmen who had not fallen victim to the scourge of range thieves or "land pirates." No doubt the ranchers who lost valuable property felt that something needed to be done to stop their losses.

Story after story about rustlers were printed in the local newspapers. One gets the sense of the magnitude of the coverage—and the mounting violence—from the following account:

A Nebulous Story.

The following s[e]nsational telegram from Miles City is published in the St. Paul Day. Take it for what you think it is worth: the fight at Mingusville between cowboys and horse-thieves was hot. Five empty saddles belonging to cowboys were found on the field. The vigilantes are said to have come from Wyoming. If so, they are bent on vengeance. There were four of the party hanged on Beaver, 17 miles north of Mingusville.[1]

Indeed, theft was a major topic of conversation during the 1884 Eastern Montana Stock Growers Convention in Miles City. The eastern Montana men, including Granville Stewart, weren't *publicly* enthusiastic about such proposals. Their reticence appeared to signal that they wouldn't take action against the thieves. In hindsight, what Stuart wanted was absolute secrecy to carry out reprisals.

One newspaper article reported:

> We learn from some of the cowboys who went with Con Kohrs' herd
> of cattle from the south fork of the Sun river [sic] to the new range
> beyond Maginnis, that horse thieves are very bad in that section of the
> country. Horses are night herded and in many cases kept under lock
> and key at night. A couple of Con Kohrs' horses were stolen, and several
> of Granville Stuart's.[2]

Judging from the noted stockmen's lack of candor even years after the
events took place, they must have held concerns that history might come
to judge them harshly. Nevertheless, they decided that time had come to
rein lawlessness in.

Many people wanted to rid Montana of the criminal element. An
article, written on July 24, 1884, captures the feelings of the local citizens:

> Horse Thieves
>
> Five horse thieves were captured and hung in the vicinity of Rocky
> point [sic] a few days ago. . . . The deed was done by a band of regularly
> organized cow boys [sic], who set out to round up the thieves that infest
> that section, and they are doing their work in good shape. They secured
> thirty-two head of horses from the quintet of outlaws, and then made
> short work of them by hanging the lot to the nearest tree. . . . The stock
> men and other citizens are making it decidedly interesting for the out-
> laws that infest the region between the lower Judith and Musselshell.
> Within the past three weeks thirteen of them have been lynched, and
> it is probable the end is not yet. The campaign was opened up by the
> killing of two thieves on the Musselshell . . . two more were "fixed" in
> Lewiston [sic] on the Fourth, and the big haul at Rocky Point is the
> latest—making in all thirteen victims. At this rate it will not take long
> to clean out the gang, and it is the only effective way to do it.[3]

At the time, there was a prevailing belief that a large, organized gang of
horse thieves existed, numbering at least one hundred strong.

Such retaliations likely were led, or at least approved, by Montana's founding father Granville Stuart. The prevailing open secret was that Stuart had assumed the leadership of a group of men banded together who became known as "Stuart's Stranglers." A man who kept meticulous records, Stuart took the role as a prominent leader.

One major shoot-out took place on the Missouri River. It came to be known as the Battle of Bates Point, and the hostilities broke out between Stuart's "Stranglers" and eleven roughs led by a man known as "Stringer Jack":

> On July 16, the vigilance committee . . . surrounded [the hideout] and found five men twenty yards south secreted in a tent, acting as watchmen. When the vigilance committee was discovered a watchman [proceeding] toward the house to give notice. The signal gun was fired, and he fell dead. An action ensued, and two of the remaining inmates of the tent were killed, one wounded, and the other escaped unhurt, Sam Jones lived two hours after receiving his mortal wound and DISCLOSED THE INTRICACIES of their work. The vigilantes, exasperated by his story, proceeded to the house and demanded the surrender of the occupants, to which Jack Stringer the leader replied: "We will lick you sons of b—s." There were but eight vigilantes against eight criminals. The former, seeing the folly of attacking their fortifications, protected by loopholes, set fire to the stable, hoping it would reach the house and oust them. Unfavorable winds delayed its progress. . . . Five are here imprisoned, three killed, and five supposed to be eighteen miles below here, including Billy Donnes. At this house the vigilantes recovered thirty-five horses and twenty-nine at Donnes', only a few miles distant.[4]

That same day, reportedly the vigilantes tracked Billy Downes (Donnes). There are conflicting accounts concerning this man's reputation, but it seems likely that he dealt in stolen goods. He was with another man named California Ed. Although the men protested that they had "only stolen horses from Indians," there were twenty-six horses with well-known brands, and none of them their own. The vigilantes found a nearby grove of cottonwood trees, and they strung the men up.

This act was not condoned by Stuart, as Downes was a "family man" and the horses may have been of little value. That said, the valuation of horses bearing other outfit's brands were never figured into the equation of whether men lived or died.

The number of men killed as horse thieves and cattle pirates in the Horse Thief War will likely never be known with certainty.

STOCK DETECTIVES AND INSPECTORS

The western states favored branding, and the usage of stock detectives was introduced as the states and territories became more settled and attempted to inject some measure of stability into the Wild West.

Taking Colorado as an example, the beginnings of the Stockgrowers Associations (including horse breeders) started off straight forward enough.

On January 18, 1868, a meeting was called to order by A. G. Reed in the chair. The president was fully authorized to employ detectives for the use and benefit of the association.

> February 1st, 1868
>
> Moved by Mr. Steele that each member brand their horses, mules and asses where they please if they want the protection of the Association, but are respectfully requested to record the same on the books of said association. Carried.[5]

This is where the story gets interesting. David J. Cook, mentioned as having arrested L. H. Musgrove, was twenty-seven years old and already serving his second term as the City Marshal of Denver. Cook was chosen by the stockmen as the right man for the job . . . or possibly the wrong one, as events transpired. The tough, shrewd, and dedicated lawman already had a string of successes underneath his belt and had recently formed the Rocky Mountain Detective Association. In those early days, it was little more than a loose agreement between Cook and other law enforcement officers throughout the territory and surrounding regions.

Cook set out at once to learn everything he could about the cattle industry, and by extension horse breeding and the rest of the livestock business. To add another wrinkle, in the beginning, he was given false and misleading information, which didn't sit well. He created a detailed report concerning the losses of each member together with explanations as to what happened to the stock and named names of people involved.

According to one account, "He prepared his report with grim humor and waited until the next meeting of the Association was in progress. He sent the document to the presiding officer and said his report might have some bearing on the heated conversation taking place."[6]

Dave Cook started reading his report. As he went on, the members of the Association became more alert. "The chief rustlers are—," and Cook named three of the officers of the association, and some of the other members.

No doubt, the meeting descended into chaos. Resignations followed swiftly—but none of them were Cook's. Cook's biographers state that the accused men made restitutions for losses.[7]

That is when the Stockgrowers Association started growing teeth.

ANTI-HORSE THIEF ASSOCIATIONS

By the 1820s, associations existed within the United States for the detection and apprehension of horse thieves specifically. Kansas joined the movement in 1868, and by 1902 there were 219 chapters of the Anti-Horse Thief Association located in that state alone. With 6,127 members on its rolls, 150 of the chapters were located in counties that bordered Missouri and the Oklahoma Territory, presenting the idea that most of their troubles came from, or headed into, those directions.[8] Missouri chapters opened in 1874, and Nebraska chapters in 1885. An act passed in 1884 that made it possible for the entire membership "upon view and without warrant, to apprehend and arrest all persons committing breaches of the peace in any township in which the society was organized."[9]

During these times of organizing, horse thieves started some of their own associations—albeit on the other side of the law. Horse thieves in the Black Hills of South Dakota formed their own association, taking what they could learn from their pursuers. "After capturing five outlaws in 1877, the army found the written 'constitution' of a large horsethief operation in the camp. Each member had been assigned a number in place of his name."[10]

It proved difficult for law enforcement to share information effectively. One response was to assign deputy US marshals who could cross jurisdictions.

The Farmers' Alliance is another interesting story. Originally organized in Lampasas County, Texas, in 1874 or 1875, it eventually became the populist party, born out of area farmers' frustrations with horse thieves and cattle rustlers.[11]

By 1916, Arkansas, Colorado, Illinois, Iowa, Kansas, Missouri, Nebraska, New Mexico, Oklahoma, Texas, and Wyoming all had Anti-Horse Thief chapters, and a membership approaching fifty thousand strong.[12] It is important to note that the Anti-Horse Thief Association did not consider itself a vigilante committee. Their motto was "Protect the innocent; bring the guilty to justice," and is interpreted to support turning the apprehended thieves over to the proper law enforcement authorities. In 1926, the Anti-Horse Thief Association changed their name to the Anti-Theft Association, but times were changing. During the 1920s, many lodges ceased operations, finding that the telephone worked wonders, that the automobile replaced the horse, and that the abilities of law enforcement had matured over the years. Still, many rural switchboards closed overnight, and of course the thieves knew this. By 1940 the group transformed more into a type of rural crime prevention society. By the end of World War II, the Anti-Horse Thief Association ceased to exist in any meaningful form.[13]

BRAND INSPECTORS

Brand inspectors are the modern equivalent to stock detectives. Straight out of the pages of the Old West, today's brand inspectors do what their predecessors did, namely inspect brands and determine ownership. It may surprise some to learn that horse theft still occurs (although reported missing horses have often simply wandered off). Either way, that's where the brand inspector comes in. A brand inspector checks the brand against ownership documents, issues travel permits, and will contact the state veterinarian if any communicable disease is suspected.

Brand inspectors are law enforcement officials, and they work closely with sheriffs. Depending upon the state, duties, details, and authority can vary. All of them will assist in the case of lost equines or outright theft.[14]

Western Horse Trivia

Colorado's Brand Board was founded in approximately 1865, when the state was still a territory, and has been in existence ever since. The division administers over thirty-two thousand brands, including horse brands.[15]

NOTES

1. *Daily Enterprise*, October 24, 1884, https://chroniclingamerica.loc .gov/lccn/sn85053382/1884-10-24/ed-1/seq-3/#date1=1880&index =15&date2=1900&searchType=advanced&language=&sequence=0&lccn=&words =Horse+horse+Horse-Thief+Thief+thief&proxdistance=5&state=Montana&rows =20&ortext=&proxtext=&phrase.

2. *River Press*, November 7, 1883, https://chroniclingamerica.loc .gov/lccn/sn85053157/1883-11-07/ed-1/seq-3/#date1=1875&index =19&rows=20&words=Con+Kohrs&searchType=basic&sequence=0&state=&date2 =1925&proxtext=%22Con+Kohrs%22&y=7&x=14&dateFilterType=yearRange&page =1.

3. Billings Gazette, "Lewistown's 1884 Fourth of July Shootout a Wild West Legend," https://billingsgazette.com/news/state-and-regional/montana/lewistown-s -1884-fourth-of-july-shootout-a-wild-west-legend/article_01679dd8-871d-11df-8f74 -001cc4c03286.html#tncms-source=login.

4. *Sun River Sun*, August 21, 1884, page 2, https://chroniclingamerica.loc.gov /lccn/sn86075197/1884-08-21/ed-1/seq-2/#date1=1862&index=0&rows =20&words=Jack+Stringer&searchType=basic&sequence=0&state=Montana&date2 =1963&proxtext=Jack+Stringer&y=0&x=0&dateFilterType=yearRange&page=1.

5. Richard Goff and Robert H. McCaffree, *Century in the Saddle: The 100 Year Story of the Colorado Cattleman's Association*, Boulder, CO: Johnson Publishing Company, 1967, 24.

6. Goff and McCaffree, *Century in the Saddle*, 30.

7. Goff and McCaffree, *Century in the Saddle*, 31–33.

8. John K. Burchill, *Bullets, Badges, and Bridles: Horse Thieves and the Societies That Pursued Them*, Gretna, LA: Pelican Publishing Company, Inc., 2014, 22.

9. Burchill, *Bullets, Badges, and Bridles*, 39.

10. Burchill, *Bullets, Badges, and Bridles*, 47.

11. Burchill, *Bullets, Badges, and Bridles*, 57.

12. Burchill, *Bullets, Badges, and Bridles*, 135.

13. Burchill, *Bullets, Badges, and Bridles*, 164–66.

14. Colorado Department of Agriculture, "Frequently Asked Questions Re: Brand Inspection," https://ag.colorado.gov/sites/ag/files/documents/FAQ%20February%202019%20Update%20-%20FINAL%20-%20PDF.pdf.

15. Colorado Department of Agriculture, "Brands History," https://ag.colorado.gov/brands-history.

CHAPTER 10

WORK HORSES

Fire horses, Denver, Colorado, 1890s.
COURTESY OF THE DENVER FIREFIGHTERS MUSEUM

NOT SO VERY LONG AGO, HORSES HAD USES BEYOND THE RANCH AND farm. To the modern mind, mechanized motors have replaced what was once the exciting concept known as "horsepower." The origins of the term *horsepower* are as follows:

Unit for measurement of the rate at which a motor works, 1805, from horse (n.) + power (n.); established by Watt [Scottish scientist in the eighteenth and nineteenth centuries] as the power needed to lift 33,000 pounds one foot in one minute, which actually is about 1.5 times the power of a strong horse. Much abused in 19c. technical writing as "very fallacious," "shockingly unscientific," etc.[1]

Horses *were* the engines of the time. In fact, horses were a tangible part of the common workforce. In the not-so-distant past, horses fulfilled very real needs in society, in the cities, and in agricultural and ranch work. They hauled building materials (and even moved entire buildings) household contents on the migration west, plowed fields, pulled firetrucks and horse trams (the precursor to street cars), crushed ore in stone arrastras, pulled stagecoaches, carried soldiers, and the list goes on—not the least of which was herding cattle and carrying cowboys and ranchers. One little-known fact involving horses is that beer brewer market areas were determined by the distance a team of horses could haul a load of beer and be back at the brewery before nightfall![2] Unsurprisingly, the specific undertaking dictated the type of horse used, but for obvious reasons, draft horses (and multiples of draft horses) were used for the heavier loads and haulage.

The most demanding job of all, however, belonged to the firehorses.

In the earliest days of firefighting, the needed equipment was pulled by the firemen to the site of the blaze. The widely accepted year of 1860 in the United States marks the beginning of widespread horse usage by local fire departments. The age of the firefighting horses lasted until 1920. In the mountainous west, men continued to pull fire equipment into the 1870s and even beyond in some locations. In the cities and larger towns, wherever possible, the use of horses for pulling heavy equipment became widespread.

Firehorses required two full years of training before they were put to work in such a dangerous capacity. Percherons were often the preferred breed. Harnessing horses to pull the fire trucks and wagons proved to be complicated and somewhat of an artform. Larger cities, like Denver, had mechanisms that lowered the harnesses down on the Percherons to save time.³ Locating and purchasing the "right" horse could prove a difficult task requiring a good amount of judgment on the part of the procurer. Each animal had to be physically large enough to pull heavy equipment, but also agile and fleet. Depending upon the fire department in the 1860s, the fireman might have supplied his own horse for whatever wagon he drove, feeding and caring for it out of his own wages. It stands to reason that the firemen weren't necessarily trained but learned from experience. Where their horses were concerned, the same could be said. As the cities grew, the fire companies expanded. In the progression of the time, places for men to sleep were provided, along with stalls for the horses and places to keep the fire wagons—acting as a precursor to the modern fire stations of today.

The horses caught on quickly to their tasks. In San Francisco, it is said that their horses could tell the difference between a fire alarm bell

Harnessing the firehorses, circa 1901–1902.
DENVER FIREFIGHTERS MUSEUM.

and a bell to mark the time. "If the bell rang for a test, they would come leisurely out of their stalls, but if it was the fire alarm, they sprang to their feet, ready to go."[4] It is difficult to say in hindsight which was more difficult to find: the men willing to fight conflagrations, or the horses upon which so much depended:

> Selecting a horse for a fire brigade was a difficult task. Usually, only one in a hundred horses proved to be acceptable. Besides the need to be highly trainable, the work also required great strength and stamina. Lightweight horses were typically used to pull hose wagons, while middleweights pulled "steamers," the steam-powered pumpers. The largest horses, draft breeds weighing in at 1,700 pounds or more, pulled the heavy equipment, and hook-and-ladder carts. While the budgets of most fire brigades were modest, they spared little expense in acquiring the highest quality horses. Fast and reliable horses meant the difference between reaching a fire in time and getting there too late.[5]

Veterinarians were often on hand to examine the horses to determine their suitability for the tasks. The veterinarian would go over the equine carefully, testing its lungs, muscles, and legs. The horse, if found acceptable, would be placed under a probationary period to see how it handled. The equine firefighter was watched closely for traits, as to whether it was prone to stumbling, could back up easily, and whether it was trainable and adaptable in general. After determination that a specific horse was found suitable, it would be purchased. The purchase price was normally around three hundred dollars per head, a marked contrast from the ninety dollars paid for a standard cavalry horse.

After the purchase, the work of training the horse to the ways of the firehouse and fire duties commenced. A horse would be exposed to the life of a fire station—the bells, men shouting, the opening of doors, rushing around, and the like. It must have been imperative that the horses did not react or spook at sounds and loud noises. When the horse was new and uncertain, after the shouting, clanging of bells, and the rumbling of wheels and hooves clattered away, they would be left in comparative silence. This no doubt felt unsettling in the beginning of their careers.

The firemen would work with the horses to teach them to leap out of their stalls for true fire alarms and to quickly move to their harness station. Each firehorse had his specific place in the harness. Another requirement of the equines was that they be able to tolerate sparks, fanning fires, and smoke.[6]

And no matter if the horses liked crowds that the fires often drew or not, they had to be level-headed and tolerate them.

In 1895 Denver, however, there is a record of when organization failed, and the firehorses most certainly suffered as a result. The instance described in the following recounts a boiler explosion at Gumry's Hotel at Seventeenth and Lawrence Streets—a huge catastrophe with many fatalities accounted:

> Two pull-box alarms alerted the fire department. Fire Chief Julius Pearse left home so hurriedly that he arrived at the scene partially dressed. Thirty minutes later he issued a general alarm, summoning every fireman in the city. In the initial excitement, somebody forgot to remain aboard the fire wagon of South Denver Hose Company No. 2; its horses bolted and the wagon hurtled driverless up Seventeenth Street to Tremont Place, where it nearly crashed into the Brown Palace Hotel. The wagon then charged down Tremont before striking a telegraph pole at Fifteenth Street. One of the horses was so badly injured that the firemen put it down.[7]

Firehorses retired (like their human counterparts) once their service was completed. In Denver, the term used was *pensioned*. Careful records were kept of each horse, whom it was purchased from and date, the purchase price, weight, height, markings, and coloring, along with its position "such as buggy" or "Tck #4." One record observed listed the 1902 horse No. 76 as "pensioned due to age and service."

There are many tales of loyalty and willingness to work even after the horses were officially retired or pensioned. Instances are told of horses being on "vacation" from active duty who would find their way back to the station for company. Or those who were permanently "off duty" and jumped over fences to race back to the firehouse when the fire alarm rang.

Such magnificent horses surely won the love and admiration of everyone who ever saw them. Nowadays, we just get to hear about them, see them in old photos, or watch their heroics on film.

Percherons, draft horses, and other large breeds were pressed into many services. In fact, horses were used to move entire structures from one place to another with the use of skids. For example, in many places in the west, building materials were hard to find and expensive to purchase. True, there was more to the process than just assembling teams and cracking the whip with a "Giddyup!"

> First of all, the house was jacked up off its foundation and was placed on heavy wooden beams. The ends of these beams were pointed and tended to act as runners similar to those on a sleigh. A temporary wooden track was put down in the street and the greased runners slid along it. The track consisted of flat planks, supported by cross ties, similar to those used on railroad tracks.

> As the house inched along the street, the planks and ties left behind it were picked up and manually carried to the front of the house and laid down ahead of it. Numerous cross ties and planks, ready for reuse, . . . it was necessary to mount a capstan in the middle of the street. [A] capstan was anchored to some very strong objects well ahead of the house . . . anchored to trees by means of heavy chains. A pulley was fastened securely to the front of the house, probably to a cross beam between the wooden runners. One end of a very strong rope, or steel cable ran from this pulley to a tree trunk or other highly immovable object. It then went through the pulley and was wrapped around the capstan. The capstan was then turned by the horses which walked in a circle and tugged on a pole connected to the capstan. As they walked, the cable would slowly wind up on the capstan and pull the house forward . . . the horses had to step over the cable each time they encountered it.[8]

HORSES IN WESTERN MINING IN THE UNITED STATES
A similar device and theory was found in the use of arrastras in early mining. An arrastra was a type of primitive mill, used mainly for

crushing gold or silver ore. The idea behind it is that it is a circular device with a paved pit bottom. Two or more drag stones (or wheels) were attached to an arm, attached to a center post in the center of the circle. The arm could be pushed by a human or dragged by a horse or a mule. The word *arrastra* comes from the Spanish *arrastrar*, meaning to drag along the ground.

Horses were also used to transport and haul ore and mining equipment. Of particular importance was the hauling of mining timbers from where they were cut back to the mine shafts and tunnels where they were put into place. Curiously, it is difficult to find information on mine liveries established at the large mines in the western United States, but they surely were there.

DISEASE

In 1872, the horse flu epidemic nearly brought America to a halt. It spread from Canada, through the United States, and down to Central America, attacking horses and mules as it progressed. When the horses' ability to work stopped, much of everything else stopped right along with them. Now, there is some good that came out of this tragedy, and it comes in the form of gratitude to the animals who worked so hard for the nation. As Americans realized their debt to these working partners, this severe bout of equine flu gave rise to the movement to prevent animal cruelty. But more about that later.

This event is known as the Great Epizootic of 1872–1873. The term *epizootic* generally refers to an animal disease spreading at an unexpectedly high rate through a given population like an epidemic where humans are concerned.

The equine influenza first appeared outside of Toronto in September of 1872. Within days of the discovery, most of the animals in Toronto's liveries had caught the virus. The disease then spread through the area. The US government tried to suppress the spread by banning Canadian horses, but they didn't catch it in time. The US border towns became infected, and the infection spread. By December of 1872, the disease took hold, and in 1873, outbreaks occurred out West.

The symptoms of the influenza caused a rasping cough, fever, dropping ears, and sometimes staggering to the point of dropping. It is likely that four million equines were lost.[9] Depending upon the source, many animals suffered symptoms that took weeks, or even months, to subside. Some never fully recovered.

At this point in history, the theory of germs causing disease was new. Veterinarian care was still primitive, but owners of stricken horses did the best that they could by disinfecting (or cleaning) stables and providing new blankets and better food to aid in the horse's recovery. Some even tried home remedies and faith healing, with varied results. What this epidemic managed to accomplish was to drive home the fact that when horses were too sick to work, many industries and conveniences shut down. While this shutdown, or slowdown, led to shortages striking the cities and industrial centers the hardest, out West stagecoach lines stopped running, trains waited in the stations because coal supplies couldn't reach the locomotives, and saloons ran dry without beer deliveries. The overall economy plunged into a recession.

It is at this point in time that the field of veterinary science made huge strides forward. As one *New York Times* article from the time stated, "The veterinary surgeons are now run after by excited horsemen as soon as a horse shows the least sign of drooping, and home doctoring, except in rare instances, is abandoned for the skilled treatment of professionals."

In his 1963 book, *The American Veterinary Profession: Its Background and Development*, Dr. J.F. Smithcors writes: "The failure of attempts to establish veterinary schools prior to 1870 must in large part be charged to the willingness of the public to accept something less than what these schools had to offer . . . until the ravages of disease made it apparent that these self-appointed parishioners were not adequate, and certainly not representative of the veterinary profession."[10]

Additionally, significant progress was made in terms of humane treatment of horses. As the equine flu raged in New York City, a man named Henry Bergh placed himself and volunteers at intersections, stopping wagons and street cars to inspect the horses. Supported by a large inheritance, Bergh found his calling in 1866 at the age of fifty-three when he founded the American Society for the Prevention of Cruelty to Animals.

Motivated less by the love of animals than by a hatred of human cruelty, he used his wealth, connections, and literary talents to lobby New York's legislature to pass the nation's first modern anti-cruelty statute. Granted police powers by this law, Bergh and his fellow badge-wearing agents roamed the streets of New York City to defend animals from avoidable suffering.[11]

When the epizootic hit, his convictions captured the moment, forcing many Americans to consider radical new arguments about the problem of animal cruelty. Ultimately the invention of electric trolleys and the internal combustion engine resolved the moral challenges of horse-powered cities: "Bergh's movement reminded Americans that horses were not unfeeling machines but partners in building and running the modern city—vulnerable creatures capable of suffering and deserving of the law's protection."[12]

LIVERIES

In cities, towns, and civilized crossroads, livery stables were a definite horse-centered business. Judging by the following nostalgic tale mourning the passing of liveries as that era came to a close, it becomes apparent that they had acted as lynchpins in the communities they served.

Passing of the Livery Stable

In those good old days, there was always the livery stable proprietor sitting in tilted chair side of the archway, and a town character, a would-be politician, on the other, settling great problems of government, etc.

That long, low, rakish structure which, until yesterday, as it were, and as far as the memory of the average man runneth backward, abutted on the main street, or main-traveled highway thru hamlet, village, town and city, and was known to resident and stranger as a livery stable, has either passed or is rapidly passing from the scene. The passing has been so gradual as to have been scarcely noticeable. and one is surprised to realize that this institution has passed, or is in, the last stage of its passage. Few can recall exactly when the signs "Livery and Boarding Stable," "Livery and Sales Stable," "Horses for Hire and for Sale," "Carriages and Buggies for Hire," and so on, ceased to have interest, so gently have the former days merged with the present. It seems no time at all, when one begins to think about since one paused before passing a street entrance to the livery stable to let a brougham, a victoria, a landau, a fandaulet, a phaeton, a buggy, a trap or a sulky pass in or pass out. In the summertime, there was always the livery stable proprietor sitting in tilted chair on one side of the archway and a town character sitting in tilted chair on the other, and there was the physician just turning in his horse, or the preacher taking his out, or the politician calling for his "rig" or the drummer planning for a road wagon and a driver for tomorrow morning at 6: and inside there was the stamping of feet in the stalls, the munching of feed at the manger and the neigh of satisfaction, and the hard breathing of the hostler as he curried the horse that had done his mile in 2.10. Then there was the return of the Picnic outfit, and all the harnessing and unharnessing that made up the two or three hours, until the last vehicle was in, the last horse brushed down, the red light over the office window extinguished, the ward politician departed for home, and the big door closed for the night.[13]

True, this article comes with a great amount of sentimentality lamenting a passing way of life as the automobile replaced horses. But it captures the spirit of what the livery stables must have been like. They served a practical purpose for people who did not own suitable acreage for a horse or horses. Rental prices from those distant days weren't frequently published in the newspapers. Back then, like today's boarding stables, there were different options a person could purchase for their horse and buggy—hopefully, the horse being their primary concern. Full board, then as now, consisted of twice daily feedings of hay, water, and shelter. Additionally, the proprietors may have turned out a couple of times per day for exercise—providing the livery had access to such a place. Pastureland would be optimal, but in cities, corrals might have been the best available. Partial board would provide lesser accommodations or services—arrangements to be determined with the establishment. Most likely all prices paid included hay, water, and shelter. The cleaning out of the stalls fell to the men who worked there. Self-boarding would only cover suitable stable space, with the horse's owner retaining much of the responsibility for the horse's care. Buggies, wagons, and carriages could be kept in the livery unhitched if it were large enough or left nearby outside and ready for use as required.

One thing is for certain: the comings and goings of people in, around, and out of town would certainly have been noted by the people who ran the liveries—as would the conditions of the horses and their conveyances. A lot of information could likely be assembled from those basic clues. No doubt, gossip spread easily and rapidly.

A stagecoach in Yellowstone National Park in 1913. Stagecoaches were the primary mode of transportation within the park until 1917 when the use of cars and buses became widespread.
THE DEADWOOD COACH 1889. J. H. GRABILL. LIBRARY OF CONGRESS.

Western Horse Trivia

What is the name of the person who trims or shoes a horse's feet? A farrier. The practice of putting on protective hoof coverings dates from the first century.

NOTES

1. Online Etymology Dictionary, "Horsepower," https://www.etymonline.com/search?q=horsepower.

2. Frank Lessiter, *Horsepower*, Milwaukee, WI: Reiman Publications, 1977, 195.

3. Denver Firefighters Museum, "Frequently Asked Questions," https://denverfirefightersmuseum.org/faqs.

4. Natlee Kenoyer, *Western Horse Tales*, edited by Don Worster, Plano, TX: Republic of Texas Press, 1994, 140.

5. Barbara Sheridan, "Forged in Fire—When Horses Answered the Alarm," *Horse Journals*, https://www.horsejournals.com/popular/history-heritage/forged-fire-when-horses-answered-alarm.

6. Kenoyer, *Western Horse Tales*, 145.

7. *Colorado Encyclopedia*, "Gumry Hotel Explosion," https://coloradoencyclopedia.org/article/gumry-hotel-explosion.

8. *Rare Historical Photos*, "Moving Entire Houses by Horses, 1890–1910," https://rarehistoricalphotos.com/vintage-photographs-move-house-horses.

9. Tom Moates, "The Great Epizootic," American Quarter Horse Association, https://www.aqha.com/-/the-great-epizootic.

10. Moates, "The Great Epizootic."

11. Ernest Freeberg, "The Horse Flu Epidemic that Brought 19th-Century America to a Stop," *Smithsonian Magazine*, December 4, 2020, https://www.smithsonianmag.com/history/how-horse-flu-epidemic-brought-19th-century-america-stop-180976453.

12. Freeberg, "The Horse Flu Epidemic."

13. *Great Divide*, "Passing of the Livery Stable," January 9, 1918, https://www.coloradohistoricnewspapers.org/?a=d&d=GRD19180109-01.2.90&srpos=2&e=-------en-20--1--img-txIN%7ctxCO%7ctxTA-Livery+stable-------0-----.

CHAPTER 11

EARLY RODEOS, FAMOUS HORSES, AND RIDING "SLICK," 1882-1920

Cowgirls at the Pendleton Roundup, 1911.
LIBRARY OF CONGRESS.

THE SMALL TOWN OF DEER TRAIL, COLORADO, CLAIMS TO BE THE HOME of the first organized rodeo in 1869. The local ranchers brought out their best bucking horses to see which man could ride the longest. The winner won a new suit of clothes and bragging rights.[1] From those humble beginnings, the first assembly of what we would think of as a true, modern rodeo came from William Frederick Cody, otherwise known as "Buffalo Bill." In 1882, Cody became the chairman of the Fourth of July celebrations in North Platte, Nebraska. After all, who could possibly have been better in that role, taking into account his much-publicized background of organizing and promoting melodramas, shows, and extravaganzas? In what would become known as the "Old Glory Blowout," Cody went further than Deer Trail's suit of clothes. He persuaded local area businessmen to offer prizes for various events: bronc-busting, shooting, roping, and riding.[2]

While informal competitions undoubtedly sprang up all over the plains wherever there were cowpokes, bucking horses, and other livestock to compete with and against, the Old Glory Blowout formalized the competitions and assured a crowd of spectators would be present.

Cody also possessed an undisputed knack for capturing the public's imagination. Prior to this showcasing of skills, cowboys were often considered uncouth, uneducated hired men who were little more than saddle tramps. Cody, along with other popular influences such as Owen Wister's *The Virginian* in 1902, separated the harsh realities of life in the saddle and cast them as something glamorous and exciting. Almost overnight, the cowboy was imbued with the romanticism of the West. And while that romanticism may or may not have extended to the horses, without the horse, a cowboy was just another man on foot.

Being the first to bring the cowboy and spectacle together, Cody can be credited with sowing the seeds of the modern-day rodeo.

Denver's Festival of Mountain and Plain began in 1895, and Cheyenne Frontier Days held their inaugural event in 1897. The Pendleton Roundup was founded in 1910 with a heavy emphasis on horsemanship. Following a successful Fourth of July celebration in 1909 that had hosted bronc riding by "Indians and Non-Indians, Indian feasts and war dances, greased pig contests, sack races, foot races and fireworks," the town of Pendleton, Oregon, was encouraged by crowd turnout and enthusiasm. Like Denver and Cheyenne, community and area leaders conceived the idea for an annual event to be known as the Pendleton Roundup. At that time, the "Let'er Buck" slogan took hold.[3]

The list of early rodeos continues. Billings, Montana, hosted their first Miles City Roundup in 1913. The Pecos Rodeo in Texas claims its beginning in 1883, and therefore by rights, bills itself as the oldest running rodeo in Texas. It also claims to be the oldest rodeo in the world.[4] Perhaps it is a matter of semantics. The Forth Worth Stock Show and Rodeo, however, disputes that claim as far as the State of Texas goes.

According to Fort Worth's organization, their first rodeo took place in 1896 and thereby claims the position as the "oldest continuously running livestock show and rodeo in the state."[5]

Competition regarding legacies remains stiff in the rodeo world.

The Pecos Rodeo has been held each June since 1930. Perhaps in some years rodeos weren't held, thus enabling Fort Worth's claim.

Regardless of lineage, rodeo formats remain roughly the same whether they are huge events or smaller, regional competitions. For the uninitiated, rodeos are typically held in oval arenas to avoid livestock "cornering." There are metal pens along the longest side of the arena

O'Donnell on Whirlwind. Cheyenne Frontier Days, 1911. Union Pacific Railroad.
LIBRARY OF CONGRESS.

to hold the rough stock horses or bulls. In the pens, riders can lower themselves onto the rough stock's backs for the competition. The "timed" events, meaning the barrel racing, roping, and bulldogging competitions, enter the arena from the right of the shoots at the top of the oval. But more about that later. The penned areas are located at the bottom of the area for the livestock to leave. There are holding areas where they are gathered before release back into the contractor's pens.

The five main categories of competitive rodeo are the "rough stock" and the "timed events." The rough stock events include saddle bronc, bareback bronc, and bull riding. The timed events cover calf roping, steer wrestling, team roping, steer roping, and barrel racing.

These disciplines, with the exception of bull riding, involve horses in one or more capacities.

Saddle bronc riding is considered the "cornerstone" of the rodeo and is invariably referred to by each announcer as "the classic event" of the program. The duration of the ride is required to last eight seconds. Should the rider become unseated (fall off) before the timer's buzzer sounds, he gets no score for that ride. Of course, there is more to it than just lasting out the eight seconds. The bronc is tacked (or outfitted) with a Professional Rodeo Cowboy Association (PRCA)–modified western saddle with stirrups. A brilliant description by John Branch is as follows:

> A bucking saddle is different than a riding saddle. There was no horn, and the stirrup leathers came out of the front, not straight off the side. It attached to the horse in two places. A wide, multi-roped cinch went under the horse's chest behind the front legs. It was connected to the saddle on each side by a thin, supple leather strap called a latigo, which was drawn tight through rings until it ran out of length and was tied off. A back cinch, snugged tight with the buckles, wrapped just behind the low part of the horse's belly. The thin end of a six-foot rein clipped to a halter on the horse's head. The other end was a thick and loose weave, almost frayed, to give the rider something meaty and soft to hold inside a clenched fist.
>
> The key calculation for every ride was how much rein to give. Too little, and a drop of the horse's head might pull a rider over. Too much, and the rider exited off the back or got jerked to the side.[6]

The horse wears a halter with a single six-foot braided rope rein to be held in the hand where the rein joins the halter. There is also a flank strap known as the bucking strap, which is released from the horse as soon as possible after the ride is completed. The flank strap does not hurt the animal but simply acts as a cue that it is time for the horse to start bucking.

Each rodeo has two judges who score both the rider and the horse. Each judge controls twenty-five points for the rider and twenty-five for the horse, for a total of fifty points per judge. The contestant can earn up to twenty-five points per judge, and the horse can earn the same for a total of one hundred points, which would be a perfect score.

The rider has additional style points to consider beyond staying seated. His free hand, usually the left, remains free for the entire ride. That free hand must be held "clear," or away from the animal and his own body at all times during those critical eight seconds. The higher and more fluid that free hand is held, usually the better the score. The rider must have his spurs over the break of the horse's shoulders up toward the neck (known as the mark out position). Spurring is critical to the rider's score. Other factors considered in the overall scoring are the cowboy's control throughout the ride, the length of his spurring stroke, and how hard the horse bucks. Model spurring begins with the mark out position, sweeping to the back of the saddle (or cantle) as the horse bucks. The rider then snaps his feet back to the horse's neck a split second before the animal's front feet hit the ground.[7] Timing and rhythm are everything. The rider is scored on how well he uses his feet in spurring the horse, and a steady, rhythmic spurring is preferred. The rider will be disqualified for being bucked off before the eight-second buzzer sounds, changing hands on the rein, or touching the animal, touching himself, losing a stirrup, or touching the equipment with his spare (free) hand.

The horse is judged on its bucking pattern—spinning is particularly difficult—and power. The rider is scored on his strength, control, and spurring action.

The pickup men ride alongside the contestant, who will let go of his horse once the timer sounds and dismount, usually by grasping one of the pickup men around the waist, before lowering (or dropping) down to the ground. Being a pickup man is no easy task. The pickup rider must be able to sit his mount well, be able to ride alongside a kicking horse, and be able to stay firmly in his own saddle as the contestant grabs him with much of his weight before releasing.

The scoring is a combined score, reflecting both the rider and the horse. Riders "draw" their horses for the competition, and some horses are preferred over others. A score between seventy and eighty is considered "good." Scores in the nineties are rare and considered exceptional. The highest score in the pro circuit is 95.5 as of this writing for Logan Hay in 2022.[8] A perfect score has never (yet) been awarded in a professional rodeo.

Bareback follows much of the bronc riding rules. As the name implies, there is no saddle this time around, and all the rider has is "rigging," which is a handhold made of leather and rawhide.

Bull riding has its own association with similar rules. However, pickup men are not used in this event; rather, rodeo clowns are employed to distract bulls away from riders as needed.

Steer wrestling is another category where there are two mounted men: the wrestler and the hazer, who keep the steer running straight. This is a "fastest time" event. The steer is released from the chute; the wrestler and the hazer wait behind a barrier for the steer to claim a proper head start. The wrestler rides on the left of the steer, and the hazer rides on the right. When the wrestler's horse pulls even with the steer, the man leans over and grabs the steer's horns when they are within reach. At that point, he frees himself from his horse and plants his feet on the ground, digging his heels in to come to a stop. As the steer slows, the wrestler turns the steer's head upwards, flipping the animal onto his back. The quicker this all can be accomplished, the better the score. The clock stops when the steer's four legs are all pointed in the same direction.

A steer wrestler can become disqualified if he fails to bring the steer to a stop or fails to change the steer's running direction. There are penalties as well. The steer will trip a barrier, signaling that the horse can move forward. If the horse "jumps" that sensor, there is a ten-second penalty applied to the overall time, usually precluding the team from winning.[9]

Team roping involves horses and two positions known as the "header" and the "heeler." This is another "lowest" or "fastest" time events. The header makes what is known as a legal catch on the steer. There are three legal catches. The first is to "catch" both horns. The second is to catch around one horn and the head (referred to as a half-head), and the third is around the neck. Any other type of catch is considered illegal and will lead to disqualification. After the header makes his catch, he will turn the steer to the left, so the back two legs are within sight. The heeler will attempt to rope the back two hind legs. If he catches only one leg, there is a five-second penalty. The clock stops when the ropes are taut and the horses are facing one another. American Quarter Horses are the most popular horses ridden for this type of competition. Heading horses are generally larger and stronger, displaying the strength and power to turn the steer. The heeler horses are smaller, more agile, and display quicker reactions to the steer's movements.[10]

Barrel racing was an event traditionally for females only, but it has opened to men as well. This is a timed event where the rider and their mount race against the clock. There are three barrels set up in the arena in a triangular (often called cloverleaf) pattern. The distances between the barrels can vary depending upon the arena size and fencing. The rider aims to ride the quickest cloverleaf pattern and can choose to turn either to the left or to the right barrel first. The rider then proceeds to the other side barrel which they turn around, saving the top barrel for last. They dash to that last barrel, which they loop around and gallop straight back to the finish. The fastest time wins.

The rules are that if a horse and rider team go off pattern, they will receive a "no time." Knocking over a barrel will also result in a "no time" in both divisional races and at rodeos, but knocking into a barrel that does not fall earns a five-second penalty at divisional competitions. A rocking or tipping barrel that does not fall over does not matter at a rodeo and there is no penalty.[11]

It's believed that barrel racing began as a sport in Texas during the early 1900s with the known cloverleaf pattern, as well as a race through a figure-eight pattern that dropped off in early years. Perhaps it was

Prairie Rose. The first female to compete in bronco riding in the Cheyenne Frontier Days, 1899 or 1901.

invented for cowboys to practice skill, but women were the only ones to compete in this discipline, while men went on to compete in the other rodeo events. It wasn't until the 1940s that the competition was based on speed, rather than on the appearance and horsemanship of the ladies riding. In 1948, the Girl's Rodeo Association (now the Women's Professional Rodeo Association) was formed and in 1949 the event shifted to speed.[12]

WOMEN'S EVENTS AND HISTORY

Today, the sport of rodeo has widened, allowing women competitors in women's ranch bronc riding competitions, which are now featured in many large, mainstream rodeos. This came about in 2016 after a long absence of nearly one hundred years. There is also a men's ranch bronc division likewise established in the same year. One of the primary differences between ranch and traditional rodeo competitions is that the contestant may hold the horn or a night-latch/rope. The rider will be disqualified if they double grab (grab with both hands) the horn, rein, saddle, or night latch.[13] A night latch is a strap that does not attach to the horse's face and usually goes through the swell of the gullet hole on a western saddle. Night latches originated, or at least were used, on the old cattle drives. When a cowboy would watch cattle at night, which they called "night hawking," they found that having a strap prevented them from falling off their horse if they fell asleep.[14]

Barrel racing was, until recently, the only event for women in the larger circuits. But that wasn't always the case. In the 1910s and 1920s, women rode broncs as well as the men, although in a separate competition. Back in those days, many female riders rode "hobbled," which created its own set of problems. Hobbled horses in this instance meant that the stirrups were tied under the horse's belly. This enabled stability through the upper foot and legs. When the horse bucked, the top of the boot would brace against the top of the stirrup, which helped prevent the rider from coming unseated. The problem with riding hobbled proved twofold. First, the rider couldn't kick clear of the stirrups if the horse fell. Secondly, if the ties underneath the horse snapped, the stirrups were no longer "fixed" or constrained, and the change caused a loss of balance and hurtled the rider forward and airborne, likely before they even knew what happened.

Nevertheless, the early twentieth century offered an exciting time for women on the rodeo circuit. The Wild West shows had existed for decades by this time, displaying the legendary talents of such notables as Annie Oakley and Calamity Jane. Women have always ridden horses. In the Victorian age, the preferred method used sidesaddles. A large percentage of those saddles were of the English conformation, but western sidesaddles did, and do, exist. Western sidesaddles are without the saddle horn since they would have constricted the rider's top leg. No doubt, *somewhere*, there is a western sidesaddle replete with a horn, but it would be rare. There are instances where a jumping strap or surcingle for the rider to grasp were used.

A sidesaddle has two bent heads (or pommels) configured to clasp a woman's thigh and to provide a resting brace. The top protrusion is called a fixed head, and the bottom is called the leaping head. The rider would put her left foot into the single stirrup for balance and stability and, seated facing forward, her left thigh would rest against the fixed head, allowing her to ride essentially with her legs together. The western sidesaddles had pronounced skirts and fenders to protect the woman's garments from touching the horse's coat and hair. Riding astride, during the 1800s and in some cases into the 1900s, was considered ill-bred, uncouth, and mannish in many parts of the civilized world.

That said, today the sidesaddle is making a comeback in certain specialty events, such as costumed races at the Calgary Stampede and exhibition events and competitions.

In the West, historically, usage of the sidesaddle was down to a matter of the woman's personal choice. Out on the range there were few people to gauge decorum. Women could wear trousers when they rode if desired—a strict breach of eastern formality at that time. Innovative split skirts were designed to bridge that gap, utilitarian patterns in durable material suited for chasing horses, riding the fence line, or herding cattle in the open. Those utilitarian skirts evolved into stunning, fancy skirts that many of the female performers wore in the Wild West shows.

THE WOMEN'S WILD WEST

Female riders started appearing in the Wild West shows of the 1890s to the delight of the audiences, and many competed in rodeo.

The vast majority of Wild West show participants, both male and female, were skilled horse handlers and decent, if not great, rifle shots. Some of the famous names of the time were Tillie Baldwin (who was credited as one of the first females who attempted steer wrestling), Mabel Strickland, Fanny Sperry Steele, Tad Lucas, Bonnie McCarroll, Marie Weiscamp, Alice and Margie Greenough, and May Lillie, and a host of other female riders.

May Lillie, who married Pawnee Bill, was credited with the following quote given in Chicago: "Let any normally healthy woman who is ordinarily strong screw up her courage and tackle a bucking bronco, and she will find the most fascinating pastime in the field of feminine athletic endeavor. There is nothing to compare, to increase the joy of living, and once accomplished, she'll have more real fun than any pink tea or theater party or ballroom ever yielded."[15]

Lucille Mulhall was a true cowgirl.

One of the first women to compete against men in both roping and riding events, Mulhall wore a host of appellations: Rodeo Queen, Queen of the West, Queen of the Saddle, and others, including the "first cowgirl," as was apparently bestowed upon her by none other than Teddy Roosevelt. According to legend, he told her that if she could rope a wolf, he would invite her to his inaugural parade. She came back three hours later, dragging a wolf behind.[16] She started her career with the Miller Brothers 101 Ranch Wild West Show (founded in 1893) in Ponca, Oklahoma. She formed her own troupe in 1913 and produced her own rodeo in 1916. She retired to her family's ranch in Mulhall, Oklahoma, around 1922.

The link between ranch life, the Wild West Shows and rodeo was clear from the start. In 1904, when 21-year-old Bertha Kaepernick mounted a bronc at the Cheyenne Frontier Days, her wild ride launched a new era in rodeo. Having talked her way into the event to do an exhibition ride, this Colorado cowgirl and aspiring rodeo competitor showed that women could ride broncs as well as any man. Women had been riding in Wild West exhibition shows since at least the 1890s but, until Kaepernick, none had successfully broken into one of the big rodeos.[17]

But female rodeo riders competing in the rough stock events didn't last.

Bonnie McCarroll's death at the Pendleton Roundup in 1929 closed that chapter on female bronc riding. Born Mary Ellen Treadwell in 1897 on her grandparent's ranch outside Boise, Idaho, she was already riding "buckers" at the tender age of ten. She married bulldogger Frank McCarroll in 1915, and her riding career took off when she rode at the Pendleton Roundup that same year. Bonnie captured nationwide attention as the result of a photograph taken of her being violently thrown from a horse named Silver in 1915. Since one stirrup is shown flying high in the air, it is likely that she had been riding hobbled, and the strap broke. Walter Bowman's photograph would prove to be an eerie precursor of what fate held in store for Bonnie.

She captured the saddle bronc riding title in 1921 at Madison Square Garden and again in 1922 at the Cheyenne Frontier Days. Bonnie was thrown from a horse named Black Cat in the 1929 Pendleton Roundup. She died eleven days afterwards from the injuries she sustained. Her tragic death, held as one of the reasons for banning women from the rough stock events, marked the decline of women's participation of mainstream rodeo.

Historian Mary Lou LeCompte, wrote, "The end of women's rodeo was Gene Autry. He put women in their 'place,' in the square dances and out of competition."[18]

Perhaps an overstatement, the tide turned.

Autry, who owned the largest stock contracting company in the world at the time, did not allow women bronc riders. The Cowboy Turtles Association, formed in 1936, which was the forerunner of the PRCA, also did not allow women's events.[19]

Bonnie McCarroll thrown from Silver. Although severe, this was not her fatal accident. Doubleday Neg. 215.

RODEO STOCK CONTRACTORS

Gene Autry was more than a singer or a Hollywood actor. He was born in north Texas and later worked on his father's ranch after they moved to Oklahoma. A cowboy and promoter at heart, he later became a prominent stock contractor. Autry owned a string of rodeo stock during the height of his on-screen popularity in 1941. Based north of Ardmore, Oklahoma, he owned the Flying A Ranch, which consisted of twelve hundred acres. In 1942, in addition to reporting for duty in World War II, Autry also became a partner in the World Championship Rodeo Company. That operation furnished livestock for many of the United States' major rodeos and events. That company, started by Everett E. Colburn of DeLamar, Idaho, provided the stock and produced rodeos in Idaho, Utah, and Wyoming in the 1920s and 1930s. In 1937, Colburn purchased that operation outright from Colonel W. T. Johnson of San

Antonio, together with a group of Arizona businessmen. They moved the business to Dublin, Texas, where it stayed for many years.

Meanwhile, in 1954, Autry acquired what was known as Montana's top "bucking" string from the estate of Leo J. Cremer Sr. of Melville, Montana.

Cremer's operations obviously held a history all their own. In 1919, Leo Cremer was "bitten by the rodeo bug" and had to try it out for himself. He won two back-to-back titles for bulldogging in the Livingston Rodeo. The Cremer Ranch "served as headquarters for his traveling rodeo, which he called Leo J. Cremer's World Championship Rodeo Company. While the ranch remained an active, working ranch that raised livestock, the Cremer Ranch also "raised the best string of bucking horses in the entire state of Montana. Perhaps the world."[20]

One of the differences between Cremer and other rodeo producers was that he experimented with horse breeding, introducing strong and husky horses into the rodeo arena, which in those days favored light-weight horses.

Bucking horses with names like Hoochie Coochie, Hell to Set, Widow Maker, Sad Face, Tim Buck Two, and Bald Hornet were among Cremer's best animals. One of his favorite bucking horses was a mare named Prison Bar, which Cremer so named because she was born outside of the Montana state penitentiary near Deer Lodge. Prison Bar was such a good bucker she performed in Cremer's rodeos well past her twenty-fifth birthday. Another horse named Come Apart was even better: In 1979 she was inducted into the Pro Rodeo Hall of Fame.[21]

Cremer died on November 29, 1953, as a result from injuries when his truck slid off the road.

But back to Autry.

When Autry purchased into the partnership in 1942, the name was changed to the World Championship Rodeo Company, Gene Autry and Associates. A merger within the company in 1956 made Autry the sole owner. As such, he moved the entire company to a twenty-four-thousand-acre ranch near Fowler, Colorado. He hired Canadian saddle bronc riding champion Harry Knight to manage the operations. For the next twelve years, he and Knight provided stock for most of the major rodeos in Texas, Colorado, Montana, and Nebraska. They terminated their business in 1968, although Autry and Knight stayed involved in rodeo.

Autry sold his business to the Cervi Brothers.

Mike Cervi began his rodeo career at the tender age of fourteen. He traveled the United States and Europe with Gene Autry.[22]

Today, the Cervi Rodeo Company is the country's largest rough stock supplier. Located in Stoneham, Colorado, near Sterling, their operation is located on sixty thousand acres; the horses and bulls have plenty of room to run and graze. Out of the over 650 horses the Cervi family owns, about 300 are located at the ranch. The other 350 are at another ranch in Medicine Bow, Wyoming. Currently, Cervi Rodeo Company has two hundred horses on their bucking string, and all of them will compete at the National Western Stock Show.[23]

As stands to the law of nature, livestock raising can't be rushed. The process of fostering a bucking bronc is very slow. From the time a breeding is selected, that foal will not compete in a PRCA rodeo until seven years later if they turn out to have what it takes to be a promising competitor.

FAMOUS RODEO HORSES

Steamboat (Saddle Bronc)

From 1901 to 1914, this legendary horse from the State of Wyoming was infamous for throwing riders in spectacular fashion in rodeos across North America. He was named for the noise he made after a bone in his nose was removed after an accident as a colt. A fierce animal, many cowboys attempted and did ride him, but that didn't lessen his mystique. Most Wyomingites believe Steamboat is the horse featured in their state logo, but arguments continue as to who the rider is.[24]

War Paint (Saddle Bronc)

War Paint was the product of a Quarter Horse stud and a wild Pinto mare. He was "raided" by Orie Summers on the Klamath Indian Reservation and became the greatest saddle bronc of his generation. As

Steamboat.
WYOMING STATE ARCHIVES.

part of the Christensen Brothers' string of buckers, War Paint was voted the PRCA Bucking Horse of the Year in each of the first three years the honor was bestowed, winning it outright in 1956/1957 while sharing the award with Harry Knight's Joker in 1958.[25]

High Tide (Bareback)

A direct descendent of the legendary racehorse Man O' War, High Tide was a part of the Flying U Rodeo Company until he was thirty-eight years old, the amazing equivalent of 105 human years. He first competed in the National Finals Rodeo in 1967 and was selected twenty more times, far outdistancing his equine counterparts. Named the top bareback horse of the 1975 National Finals Rodeo, he was retired at the 1986 National Finals Rodeo. High Tide was known for his consistency and attitude. The horse was described by his human athletic competitors as "one in a million."[26]

There are many, many more fabulous horses to read about and this but scratches the surface. Entire books could be devoted to wild and interesting facets of early rodeo history.

Western Horse Trivia

In 2008, Grated Coconut was voted for the fifth time the PRCA Bareback Horse of the Year. Prior to this, only one other horse accomplished this honor; his name was Skoal Sippin' Velvet. He won his last title in 1987 and was inducted into the Pro Rodeo Hall of Fame in 2000.

NOTES

1. Town of Deer Trail, "About Us," https://townofdeertrail.colorado.gov/about-us#: ~:text=Deer%20Trail%20is%20know%20as,and%20bragging%20rights%20of%20course.

2. Elizabeth Atwood Lawrence, *Rodeo: An Anthropologist Looks At the Wild and the Tame*, Knoxville, TN: University of Tennessee Press, 1982, 45.

3. Pendleton Roundup, "History," https://www.pendletonroundup.com/p/round-up /147.

4. Pecos Rodeo, "About Us," https://pecosrodeo.com/pages/history.

5. Peter Simak, "The Oldest, Biggest, Best Texas Rodeos," *Texas Heritage for Living*, https://texasheritageforliving.com/texas-living/best-texas-rodeos.

6. Lawrence, *Rodeo*, 25.

7. Spokane County, "Saddle Bronc," https://www.spokanecounty.org/1070/Saddle -Bronc.

8. Brady Renck, "Saddle Bronc Rider Logan Hay Registers World-Record 95.5-Point Win in Pollackville Win," *ProRodeo*, July 30, 2022, https://prorodeo.com/news/2022/7 /31/general-saddle-bronc-rider-logan-hay-registered-world-record-95-5-point-ride-in -pollockville-win.

9. *Post Register*, "Rules and Regulations for Steer Wrestling," https://www.postregister .com/rules-and-regulations-for-steer-wrestling/article_f0c7f553-f3f7-5a2e-9d18 -d3e5deb9e38e.html.

10. *Post Register*, "Rules and Regulations for Steer Wrestling."

11. *Barrel Racing Magazine*, "Training," https://barrelracing.com/category/training/ ?ucterms=category~barrel-racing-101.

12. Gail Hughbanks Woerner, "The History of Barrel Racing," *The Wrangler Network*, October 14, 2014, https://wranglernetwork.com/news/the-history-of-barrel-racing.

13. Women's Ranch Bronc Championships, "Women's Ranch Bronc Riding Rules," https://www.womensranchbronc.com/standings.

14. Katie Frank, "The Necessity of a Night Latch," *Western Horseman*, June 28, 2019, https://westernhorseman.com/horsemanship/gear/the-necessity-of-a-night -latch/#:~:text=Night%20latches%20can%20often%20be%20seen%20in%20the ,leap%20a%20lot%20better%20and%20keep%20you%20balanced.%E2%80%9D

15. Kathy King Johnson, "History of the Opera House Part 53: Pawnee Bill and May Lillie," *Cheboygan Daily Tribune*, July 27, 2021, https://www.cheboygannews.com /story/opinion/2021/07/27/history-opera-house-part-53-pawnee-bill-and-may-lillie /8091164002.

16. Joyce Gibson Roach, "Mulhall, Lucille (1885– 940)," The Oklahoma Historical Society, https://www.okhistory.org/publications/enc/entry.php?entry=MU006.

17. Cindy Hirschfeld, "Ride like a Girl: The Original Rodeo Cowgirls," *American Cowboy*, July 14, 2022, https://americancowboy.com/cowboys-archive/ride-girl.

18. Hirschfeld, "Ride Like a Girl."

19. Jim Olson, "Bonnie McCarroll—End of an Era," *Triple A Livestock Report*, https:// www.aaalivestock.com/bonnie-mccarroll-end-of-an-era.

20. Todd Klassy, "Leo J. Cremer: the Rodeo King of Montana's Historic Cremer Ranch," *Distinctly Montana*, September 13, 2023, https://www.distinctlymontana.com/ leo-j-cremer-rodeo-king-montanas-historic-cremer-ranch.

21. Klassy, "Leo J. Cremer."

22. Cervi Championship Rodeo, "Meet the Family that Has Lived Out the Rodeo Life Aa All Different Angles," http://cervirodeo.com/projects.

23. Robyn Scherer, "Cervi Rodeo Company Produces Superior Bucking Stock," *The Fence Post*, January 9, 2012, https://www.thefencepost.com/news/cervi-rodeo-company -produces-superior-bucking-stock.

24. Cheyenne Frontier Days, "About Us," https://cfdrodeo.com/about%20us.

25. Pro Rodeo Hall of Fame, "War Paint," https://www.prorodeohalloffame.com/ inductees/livestock/war-paint.

26. Pro Rodeo Hall of Fame, "High Tide," https://www.prorodeohalloffame.com/ inductees/livestock/high-tide.

CHAPTER 12

WESTERN ROOTS

Horse and cattle on the range, Meeteetse area, by Belden.
WYOMING STATE ARCHIVES.

NOTHING SAYS THE WEST LIKE THE AMERICAN QUARTER HORSE.
The American Quarter Horse was a cross between the colonial quarter racehorse and Mustang or American Indian stock. These horses possess a tremendous amount of "cow sense" and feature widely today as cattle horses and in rodeos. Intelligent and willing to work, their strong hindquarters provide great bursts of speed.

> This was the horse that broke prairie sod where farms would be, carried buffalo hunters across the Llano Estacado, and made up the remudas of cow outfits from the Rio Grande to the open ranges of Alberta. It was a horse ideally suited by physique and temperament to the challenge and hardship of winning the West.[1]

THE FOUNDATION OF THE AMERICAN QUARTER HORSE

The origins of the American Quarter Horse are a bit tangled. The name, or term, *Quarter Horse*, refers to its great speed and ability to run one-quarter of a mile.

Some breed historians trace the origins of the Quarter Horse back to colonial America along the eastern coast. The term *breed* is a loosely used description of an animal capable of reproducing its characteristics, or "race, lineage, stock from the same parentage"[2] as referring to horses and other animals. Because of the colonists' interest in what was termed "short horses"—meaning racing—Thoroughbreds were imported from England to improve the speed of the American (or colonial) short-horses. The famous Janus was brought over from England in 1752, after becoming lame and unfit for racing. He was purchased prior to the English Stud Book's establishment so is not listed there, but he is found within the pages of Patrick Nesbitt Edgar's *The American Race-Turf Register Sportsman Herald and General Stud Book* of 1833.[3]

Some early sires contributed to both Thoroughbreds and the Quarter Horses, tangling the bloodlines further.

While those colonial beginnings remain one option, there is another. It is, perhaps more likely, that the true origins of what today is considered a Quarter Horse came from the American Southwest range country, where the agility, strength, and "cow-smarts" were widely appreciated.

Many modern breed historians believe that the "principle development of the Quarter Horse came from Texas, Oklahoma, New Mexico, eastern Colorado and Kansas."[4] The origins of some of the Quarter Horses are murky, and the unknown breeding of some of the horses into the 1940s make those early foundations more of a type, rather than a breed, until the Stud Book was established, basing pedigree on fact, rather than memory and recollection.

That all said, cowboys wanted good horses. Ranchers wanted to breed horses that served their purpose—namely dealing with cattle. Fast horses whose offspring made good cow ponies were highly prized, both for work and likely for open-racing sport racing. One of the American Quarter Horse Association's books, *They Rode Good Horses*, sums up the first fifty

Detail of a saddle.
LIBRARY OF CONGRESS.

years of the history of the Quarter Horse and their relationship to the cowboys and ranchers who rode them.

The heyday of the Quarter Horse breed from the mid-1800s to the early 1900s produced legendary stallions in the west. Steel Dust, for example, was foaled in Kentucky in early 1843 and moved to Texas in 1853.[5] Steel Dust is often singled out as the first western Quarter Horse. He earned a name for himself and a correspondingly high reputation on account of his racing prowess at the quarter mile. Because of his fame and skill, his progeny was much sought after in the days of the early west. Cowboys specifically sought them out, and often those early Quarter Horses were referred to as "Steel Dusts."

> A blood bay, Steel Dust was named for a rust-colored iron preparation common in 19th-century medical concoctions. It was also known as anvil dust and worn in charms to bring luck at gambling, just as the horse brought together the two most dominant lines of Celebrated American Quarter Of A Mile Running Horses, those of Janus and Sir Archy (TB). Steel Dust emerged the classic bulldog Quarter Horse: a powerfully muscled, short-coupled sprinter that stood 15 hands (or so) and weighed 1,200 pounds (or so), a lot of horse in a compact package, topped with bulging jaws and fox ears.[6]

One can't help but notice the volume of famous Quarter Horses that involve the state of Texas. Beyond Steel Dust, there is Shiloh (foaled in Tennessee in 1844 and brought to Texas in 1849, another descendant of the famed Sir Archy, born and bred in Virginia in 1805). Steel Dust lived on Ten Mile Creek in Lancaster, southeast of Dallas. In 1855, a famous race pitting Steel Dust against Shiloh was set up to run. Steel Dust was hurt at the starting gate and was unable to run. Prior to that injury, Steel Dust was said to be so fast that the jockey had to put molasses on his coat to stay on.[7]

A nostalgic accounting of that fateful day those two famous horses met was written by Wayne Gard: "The former haunts of Steel Dust still are horse country. On stormy nights some of those who live on Ten Mile Creek may think they hear his whinny—and an answering neigh from Old Shiloh on Bear Creek. If the two stallions could break away from their equine Valhalla, undoubtedly they would come back some night and finish that race of 1855, and thus settle for all time the question of which was the fleeter."[8]

The list goes on and on.

There was Billy (1860), who founded the Billy strain of horses. Known as Billy, Old Billy, Billy Boy, or Billy Fleming, he was a Shiloh/ Steel Dust cross. A foundation sire, Old Billy was a son of Shiloh, out of Steel Dust's daughter Ram Cat. He established Quarter Horses down in South Texas, a region that was sometimes referred to as "the land of the Billys."[9]

Old Billy received his name from his second owner, William B. "Billy" Fleming from Belmont, Texas. William Fleming had quite a history, and so did his horse. William Fleming was reportedly an American Indian fighter, and when he came to Texas, he enlisted in Company C of the Texas Rangers Mounted Volunteers. Later, he would fight in the Confederate Army and received a wound resulting in his inability to write. Apparently, the wound involved his right hand because he could only scribble left-handed afterwards. Due to that limitation, he was able to keep no records except "what he dictated to interested breeders and then signed with a scribble."[10] According to legend, Billy was kept chained to a tree while his original owner fought in the Civil War. When Fleming bought Billy, reportedly the horse was in "sorry shape. His hoofs were so long they had to be sawed off, and the scar from the chain on his neck was never lost, nor did that area ever grown hair again."[11] One can only hope that is a gross exaggeration passed into legend. Be that as it may, Fleming moved to Gonzales County, where he partnered with Charles Erasmus Littlefield in 1871. Old Billy was used to breed a line of Quarter Horses known as the Billys.[12]

Peter McCue (foaled February 23, 1895, and bred by Samuel Watkins at the Little Grove Stock Farm of Petersburg, Illinois) is really the powerhouse (or power horse) of the modern-day Quarter Horses, especially prominent between the years 1900 and 1940. Samuel Watkins also bred the famed Dan Tucker. Dan Tucker was a product of the very swift mare Butt Cut; Barney Owens was his sire. He was purchased by Trammel and Newman of Sweetwater, Texas. Perhaps the most famous of all the Quarter Horse sires, Peter McCue started out life registered as a Thoroughbred, but evidence later came to light that he was not sired by the horse on his official pedigree papers, but was a product of Dan Tucker, who traced his line to Shiloh.

Peter McCue's fame first came as a sprinter on the racetrack. His speed was phenomenal, and he spent much of his time in the area around San Antonio. When Peter was in that area, he was owned by John Wilkins, who later sold him to Milo Burlingame of Oklahoma. He was then sold on to Coke T. Roberds of Hayden, Colorado, who kept the stallion until he died in 1923 at the age of twenty-eight.[13]

Peter McCue stood for service in Texas, western Oklahoma, and in Colorado, and most modern Quarter Horses trace to him. Of the 11,510 Quarter Horses that were registered prior to January 1, 1948, 2,304 of them traced in male line to Peter McCue through his sons, grandsons, and great-grandsons. Traveler was the only horse that approached him in importance of male lines with 749 similar descendants that has been registered up to that date.[14]

OTHER NOTABLE QUARTER HORSES

Other notable Quarter Horses include Midnight (known as the world's greatest bucking horse foaled in 1915 in Alberta, Canada), Joe Hancock (foaled in 1923 in Perryton, Texas), Oklahoma Star (foaled in 1915 in Oklahoma), Joe Reed (foaled 1921 in Cameron, Texas), and My Texas Dandy (foaled in 1927, although some other sources state 1928, from Ellinger, Texas, and owned by the C. F. Meyers family). When it became apparent that My Texas Dandy would not make a good racehorse, he was sold to J. C. Smith, who took him out to his father's ranch in Big Foot, Texas.[15] While these horses became the foundation sires for the Quarter Horse breed, they are also the foundation for many of today's working ranch horses.[16]

WILD AND FERAL HORSES

The definition and differences between truly wild and feral horses turn out not to be cut and dried. Talk to local ranchers, environmentalists, historians, horse lovers, you name it, and there are no definitive answers.

The largest "wild horse herds" in the United States are located in Nevada, but most experts apply the term *feral* to the animals.

In 1971, when about seventeen thousand feral horses were left, the US Wild Free-Roaming Horse and Burro Act mandated the protection of these animals as "national heritage species. . . . As to what percentage are descendants of the original mustangs, and which are more recent domestic escapees . . . nobody knows."[17]

Wild (or feral) horses range in Arizona, California, Colorado, Idaho, Montana, New Mexico, Nevada, Oregon, Wyoming, and Utah.[18] When World War I ended and the market fell out for horses, many ranchers simply turned them loose, which created problems. The history of the feral horse in the twentieth century is distressing and problematic. The following article, written in 1926, outlines some of the issues encountered.

HORSE BOOTLEGGING IS NEW INDUSTRY IN WAR ON "FUZZTAILS"

Round-Up Gangs Make Little Distinction Between Wild and Tame Animals.

By GEORGE D. CRISSEY.

(United Press Staff Correspondent.) PORTLAND, Ore., Dec, 3.— (United Press.)—Illicit trafficking in liquor has a new rival—that of bootlegging horses, a practice which has developed along with the problem of eliminating the wild horse or "fuz tail," from the range lands of eastern Oregon and Washington, Idaho, Montana and Wyoming. In the brave days of long ago, when the West was wild, wicked and womenless [sic], it was a capital crime to toss your lariat over the neck of a steed belonging to another man. The customary manner of registering disapproval of such an act was to loop a rope around the neck of the horse thief and hang him from a convenient tree to swing in the breeze and furnish food for crows and buzzards. The only consolation was that in the juniper country trees of the proper size are few and far between. . . . A horse thief or horse bootlegger, attracts less attention than would an "old-fashioned girl." . . . Old Dobbin, as the plainsmen know him, lost much of his attraction in the wake of the world war as the value of an unbroken "broom tail" crashed . . . the problem is not wild horses, rather one of controlling domestic horses gone wild, and herein lies factor of horse bootlegging. During the war horses were valued and every animal capable of wearing a saddle found a ready market with the warring nations of Europe. . . . Horses became a unit of value, more an ever before; ranchers borrowed money on their free-running stock. Then came the armistice and the collapse of the value of horses. Banks found that $10,000 of wartime horse security had faded to less than the cost of catching the livestock—the horseman and rancher made the same discovery. Horses were abandoned by the hundreds, and being half wild already, it was not long before bands were formed and the branded animals roamed the plains as though their ancestors had never known halter, bridle or saddle. . . . Horse bootlegging is this: . . . the abandoned animals as well as the wild ones are being rounded up . . . and on the part of many there is no wild-eyed effort to identify owner-ship of horses rounded up. They grab all in sight, including some having owners—and therefore, the term *horse bootlegging* sprang into use. But, like liquor bootlegging in many quarters, no one cares a whole lot, so nothing much is done about it.[19]

The Pryor Mountain Mustangs in Lovell, Wyoming, and into Montana are a special breed of Mustangs. Often claimed to be the closed variant to Spanish Mustangs, the wild free-roaming horses inhabiting the Pryor Mountain Wild Horse Range most likely descend from a mixture of many domestic breeds. Recent genetic tests concluded that Pryor horses include a higher-than-average level of ancestry from New World "Span-ish" breeds (saddle type horses) and related to European "Spanish" breeds, in addition to other "light racing and riding breeds." Other genetic analyses suggested that the single closest breed to Pryor horses was the Quarter Horse. Some of the Pryor horses carry a rare allele variant *Qac* that has been traced back to the original New World "Spanish" type horses: Spanish and Portuguese (Iberian) horses that were brought to the Americas. However, all of the genetic markers in these wild horses are found in other horse breeds.[20]

Desert Dust (Mustang).
WYOMING STATE ARCHIVES.

NOTES

1. American Quarter Horse Association, "The History of the American Quarter Horse Breed," taken from Don Hedgpeth, *They Rode Good Horses: The First Fifty Years of the American Quarter Horse Association*, https://www.aqha.com/history-of-the-quarter-horse.

2. Online Etymology Dictionary, "Breed," https://www.etymonline.com/word/breed#etymonline_v_17087.

3. Patrick Nisbett Edgar, *The American Race-Turf Register Sportsman Herald and General Stud Book: Containing the Pedigrees of the Most Celebrated Horses, Mares, and Geldings That Have Distinguished Themselves on American Turf*, New York, NY: Press of Henry Mason, 1833, 8–9.

4. Oklahoma State University, "Breeds of Livestock: Quarter Horses," https://breeds .okstate.edu/horses/quarter-horses.html.

5. Bruce Beckmann, "Quarter Horses," originally published 1952, Texas State Historical Association, https://www.tshaonline.org/handbook/entries/quarter-horses.

6. Richard Chamberlain, "Steel Dust," April 26, 2022, https://www.aqha.com/-/steel -dust-1.

7. Historical Marker Database, "Fabulous Quarter Horse Steel Dust," https://www .hmdb.org/m.asp?m=152094.

8. Wayne Gard, *The Fabulous Quarter Horse: Steel Dust The True Account of the Most Celebrated Texas Stallion*, New York, NY: Duell, Sloan & Pearce, 1958, 56.

9. Robert Moorman Denhardt, *Quarter Horses: A Story of Two Centuries*, Norman, OK: University of Oklahoma Press, 1967) 29.

10. Denhardt, *Quarter Horses*, 30.

11. Denhardt, *Quarter Horses*, 30.

12. Historical Marker Database, "William B. Fleming," https://www.hmdb.org/m.asp?m=128145.

13. Denhardt, *Quarter Horses*, 42.

14. Oklahoma State University, "The Most Influential Sire," https://breeds.okstate.edu/horses/quarter-horses.html.

15. Denhardt, *Quarter Horses*, 90.

16. *Western Horseman*, "Top 5 Ranch Horse Bloodlines," https://westernhorseman.com/culture/flashbacks/the-top-10-ranch-horse-bloodlines.

17. American Museum of Natural History, "When Is 'Wild' Actually 'Feral'?" https://www.amnh.org/explore/videos/biodiversity/takhi-mongolian-horse/article-when-is-wild-actually-feral.

18. Bureau of Land Management, "Wild Horse and Burro Maps by State," https://www.blm.gov/programs/wild-horse-and-burro/about-the-program/program-maps/maps-by-state.

19. *Rocky Mountain News (Daily)*, Volume 67, Number 339, December 5, 1926, https://www.coloradohistoricnewspapers.org/?a=tc&d=RMD19261205-01.2.412&srpos=1&e=-------en-20--1--img-txIN%7ctxCO%7ctxTA-Wyoming+Horse+Thief+War-------0-----.

20. Bureau of Land Management, "Pryor Mountains Wild Horse Range," https://www.blm.gov/programs/wild-horse-and-burro/herd-management/herd-management-area/montana-dakotas/pryor#:~:text=Today%2C%20the%20Pryor%20Mountain%20Wild,northern%20Big%20Horn%20County%2C%20Wyoming.

GLOSSARY OF TERMS

Bay: Reddish brown or brown coat with black mane, tail, and legs.

Blooded: A horse of good descent. Tended to refer to English thorough-bred racehorses. Can refer to a breed originating from English mares and Arabian stallions widely favored for racing in the eighteenth and nineteenth centuries.

Blue roan: Black coat with black face, head, legs, mane, and tail, while the body takes on a bluish or grayish appearance.

Cavalcade: A procession or a parade on horseback, or the mass partici-pation of trail riders. The emphasis is on participation, rather than display (such as finery or costumes).

Cavy or cavvy: A group of ranch horses. Similar to a remuda.

Conformation: The horse's skeleton, muscles, and overall appearance.

Mochila: A Pony Express mochila was a removable lightweight leather cover put over a horse saddle for carrying mail. Unlike a saddlebag, the mochila had holes cut out for the saddle cantle and horn. There were four pockets on the mochila, which could (and should) be kept locked. Three of those pockets could only be opened at specific military posts: Forts Kearney, Laramie, Bridger, and Churchill, and at Salt Lake City. The fourth pocket could be opened by a station master at any of the other stations and held a time-card to record riders' arrival and departure times.

Remount: Military definition; the provision of fresh horses to replace those killed or injured in battle.

Remuda: Herd of saddle-broken horses used for ranch work. The word is of Spanish origin meaning "remount," although in ranching terms it is a string of available horses for the ranch hands and cowboys.

Roan: White coat color with intermixed white and colored hairs on the body. The face, head, lower legs, and tail are colored.

Rough stock: Horses and bulls bred to buck for use in rodeos. Saddle bronc, bareback, and bull riding are the disciplines using "rough stock."

Saddle horn: Part of the western saddle that protrudes in front (pommel) with the primary purpose of holding a rope to stop animals.

Saddle cantle: Back of a saddle's seat.

BIBLIOGRAPHY

PRINT

Abbott, E.C. "Teddy Blue," and Smith, Helena Huntington. *We Pointed Them North: Recollections of a Cowpuncher.* Norman, OK: University of Oklahoma Press, 1986.

Agnew, Jeremy. *Life of a Soldier on the Western Frontier.* Missoula, MT: Mountain Press Publishing Company, 2008.

Aiton, Arthur Scott. *Antonio de Mendoza, First Viceroy of New Spain.* Durham, NC: Duke University Press, 1927.

Amaral, Anthony A. *Comanche: The Horse that Survived the Custer Massacre.* Los Angeles, CA: Westernlore Press, 1961.

Bennett, Deb. *Conquerors: The Roots of New World Horsemanship.* Solvang, CA: Amigo Publications, 1998.

Berry, Rachel. "Breed of Livestock—Cayuse Indian Pony," http://afs.okstate.edu/breeds/horses/cayuseindian/index.html/.

Bourke, John G. *On the Border with Crook.* New York: Charles Scribner's Sons, 1891.

Branch, John. *The Last Cowboys: A Pioneer Family in the New West.* New York, NY: W.W. Norton & Company, 2018.

Burchill, John K. *Bullets, Badges and Bridles: Horse Thieves and the Societies That Pursued Them.* Gretna, LA: Pelican Publishing Company, Inc., 2014.

Catlin, George. *Letters and Notes on the Manners, Customs and Conditions of the North American Indians: Written During Eight Years of Travels Among the Wildest Tribes of Indians in North America.* London, England: Tilt and Bogue Fleet Street, 1842.

Chapman, Arthur. *The Pony Express; The Record of a Romantic Adventure in Business.* New York, NY: Cooper Square Publications, 1971. Originally published 1932.

Collins, Dabney Otis. *Great Western Rides.* Denver, CO: Sage Books, 1961.

Corbett, Christopher. *Orphans Preferred: The Twisted Truth and Lasting Legend of the Pony Express.* New York, NY: Broadway, 2003.

DeFelice, Jim. *West Like Lightning: The Brief, Legendary Ride of the Pony Express.* New York, NY: William Morrow, 2018.

Denhardt, Robert Moorman. *Quarter Horses: A Story of Two Centuries.* Norman, OK: University of Oklahoma Press, 1967.

De Steiguer, J. Edward. *Wild Horses of the West: History and Politics of America's Mustangs.* Second edition. Tucson, AZ: University of Arizona Press, 2011.

Diaz del Castillo, Bernal. *True History of the Conquest of New Spain.* Volume 1. London, England: J. Hatchard and Son, 1844.

Dobie, J. Frank. *The Mustangs.* Edison, NJ: Castle Books, 1952.

Dutson, Judith. *Storey's Illustrated Guide to 96 Horse Breeds of North America.* North Adams, MA: Storey Publishing, 2005.

Edgar, Patrick Nisbett. *The American Race-Turf Register Sportsman Herald and General Stud Book: Containing the Pedigrees of the Most Celebrated Horses, Mares, and Geldings That Have Distinguished Themselves on American Turf.* New York, NY: Press of Henry Mason, 1833.

Edwards, Elwyn Hartley. *The Horse Encyclopedia.* London, England: DK Publishing, 2016.

Essen, Emmett M. III. *Western Horse Tales.* Edited by Don Worcester. Plano, TX: Republic of Texas Press, 1994.

Gard, Wayne. *The Fabulous Quarter Horse: Steel Dust the True Account of the Most Celebrated Texas Stallion.* New York, NY: Duell, Sloan & Pearce, 1958.

Goff, Richard, and McCaffree, Robert H. *Century in the Saddle: The 100 Year Story of the Colorado Cattleman's Association.* Boulder: Johnson Publishing Company, 1967.

Golliher, Grant. *Think Like a Horse: Lessons in Life, Leadership and Empathy from an Unconventional Cowboy.* New York: G.P. Putnam's Sons, 2022.

Haines, Frances. *Appaloosa: The Spotted Horse in Art and History.* Austin: The University of Texas Press, 1963.

Hämäläinen, Pekka. *Indigenous Continent: The Epic Contest for North America.* New York: Liveright Publishing Corporation, 2022.

Hämäläinen, Pekka. *Lakota America: A New Indigenous Power.* New Haven: Yale University Press, 2019.

Horse Capture, George P., and Her Many Horses, Emil. *A Song for the Horse Nation: Horses in Native American Cultures.* Wheat Ridge, CO: Fulcrum Publishing, 2006.

James, Gen. Thomas. *Three Years Among the Indians and the Mexicans.* St. Louis, MO: Historical Society, 1916.

Kenoyer, Natlee. *Western Horse Tales.* Edited by Don Worster. Plano, TX: Republic of Texas Press, 1994.

Lawrence, Elizabeth Atwood. *His Very Silence Speaks: Comanche—The Horse Who Survived Custer's Last Stand.* Detroit, MI: Wayne State University Press, 1989.

Lawrence, Elizabeth Atwood. *Rodeo: An Anthropologist Looks at the Wild and the Tame.* Knoxville, TN: The University of Tennessee Press, 1982.

Leonard, Stephen J. *Lynching in Colorado 1859–1919.* Louisville, CO: University Press of Colorado, 2002.

Lessiter, Frank. *Horsepower.* Milwaukee, WI: Reiman Publications, 1977.

Luce, Edward Smith. *Keogh, Comanche and Custer.* Buffalo Grove, IL: John S. Swift Company, Inc., 1939.

Luckett, Matthew S. *Never Caught Twice: Horse Stealing in Western Nebraska, 1850–1890.* Lincoln, NB: University of Nebraska Press, 2020.

Majors, Alexander. *Seventy Years on the Frontier*. Chicago, IL: Rand, McNally and Company Publishers, 1893.

McCord, Monty. *Calling the Brands: Stock Detectives in the Wild West*. Guilford, CT: A TwoDot Book, 2018.

Medicine Crow, Joseph. *Counting Coup: Becoming a Crow Chief on the Reservation and Beyond*. Washington, DC: National Geographic, 2003.

Pony Boy, Gawani. *Horse Follow Closely: Native American Horsemanship*. Irvine, CA: Bow Tie Press, 1998.

Price, Steve. *America's Wild Horses: The History of the Western Mustang*. New York, NY: Skyhorse Publishing, 2017.

Propst, Nell Brown. *The South Platte Trail: The Story of Colorado's Forgotten People*. Boulder, CO: Pruett Publishing, 1989.

Raulff, Ulrich. *Farewell to the Horse: A Cultural History*. New York, NY: Liveright Publishing Corporation, 2017.

Ryden, Hope. *American's Last Wild Horses: The Classic Study of the Mustangs—Their Pivotal Role in the History of the West, Their Return to the Wild, and the Ongoing Efforts to Preserve Them*. Essex, CT: Lyons Press, 1999.

Sanders, Alvin Howard, and Dinsmore, Wayne. *A History of the Percheron Horse*. Chicago, IL: Breeders Gazette Print, 1917.

Sprague, Marshall. *Massacre: The Tragedy at White River*. Lincoln, NB: University of Nebraska Press, 1957.

Trask, Kerry A. *Black Hawk: The Battle for the Heart of America*. New York, NY: A John Macrae Book (Henry Holt and Company), 2006.

Turner, Erin (Ed.). *Cowgirls: Stories of Trick Riders, Sharp Shooters, and Untamed Women*. Guilford, CT: TwoDot Books, 2009.

Unknown. *Supplement to the Lecture on the Mountain Meadows Massacre: Important Additional Testimony Recently Received*. Salt Lake City, UT: printed at Juvenile Instruction Office, 1885.

Vargas Machuca, Bernardo. *The Indian Militia and Description of the Indies*. Durham, NC: Duke University Press, 2008.

Visscher, William Lightfoot. *A Thrilling and Truthful History of the Pony Express; or, Blazing the Westward Way, and Other Sketches and Incidents of Those Stirring Times*. Chicago, IL: Rand McNally, 1908.

ONLINE SOURCES

American Indian Partnership. http://www.americanindianpartnership.com/blackfeet-timeline.html.

American Museum of Natural History. http://www.amnh.org/explore/science-bulletins/bio/documentaries/the-last-wild-horse-the-return-of-takhi-to-mongolia/article-when-is-wild-actually-feral.

American Quarter Horse Association. "The Cowboy's Horse," https://www.aqha.com//the-cowboy-s-horse-1.

Appaloosa Museum. "History of the Appaloosa," http://www.appaloosamuseum.com/history-of-theappaloosa.

Ashfall.unl.edu. "From Waterhole to Rhino Barn," https://ashfall.unl.edu/about-ashfall/waterhole-to-rhino-barn.html.

Barrel Racing Magazine Online. https://barrelracing.com/category/training/?ucterms=category~barrel-racing-101.

Bureau of Land Management. https://www.blm.gov/blog/2021-03-10/kittie-wilkins-idahos-horse-queen; https://www.blm.gov/programs/wild-horse-and-burro/about-the-program/program-maps/maps-by-state; https://www.blm.gov/programs/wild-horse-and-burro/herd-management/herd-management-area/montana-dakotas/pryor#:~:text=Today%2C%20the%20Pryor%20Mountain%20Wild,northern%20Big%20Horn%20County%2C%20Wyoming.

Cervi Championship Rodeo. http://cervirodeo.com/projects.

Cheyenne Frontier Days. https://cfdrodeo.com/about_us.

Colorado Department of Agriculture. https://ag.colorado.gov/sites/ag/files/documents/FAQ%20February%202019%20Update%20-%20FINAL%20-%20PDF.pdf.

Colorado Encyclopedia Online. https://coloradoencyclopedia.org/article/meeker-incident; https://coloradoencyclopedia.org/article/gumry-hotel-explosion; https://coloradoencyclopedia.org/article/ute-history-and-ute-mountain-ute-tribe.

Deer Trail. https://townofdeertrail.colorado.gov/about-us#:~:text=Deer%20Trail%20is%20know%20as,and%20bragging%20rights%20of%20course.

Denver Firefighter's Museum. https://denverfirefightersmuseum.org/faqs.

Department of Defense. https://valor.defense.gov/Recipients/Army-Medal-of-Honor-Recipients.

Eatherly, Charles R. "Opened and Dedicated September 28, 1958," https://azstateparks.com/tubac/about-the-presidio/park-history.

Exploring Florida. https://fcit.usf.edu/florida/lessons/narvaez/narvaez1.htm#:~:text=Pánfilo%20de%20Narváez%20arrived%20near,he%20was%20able%20to%20control.

Farro, Shaunacy. https://www.mentalfloss.com/article/537885/facts-about-pony-express.

fcit.usf.edu. "The Misadventures of Pánfilo Narváez and Nuñez de Cabeza de Vaca," https://fcit.usf.edu/florida/lessons/narvaez/narvaez1.htm#:~:text=Pánfilo%20de%20Narváez%20arrived%20near,he%20was%20able%20to%20control.

Find A Grave. https://www.findagrave.com/memorial/39855539/james-holt-haslam.

Gade, Gene. "Who Was John 'Portugee' Phillips—the Man Who Rode 263 Miles to Save Fort Phil Kearney," December 21, 2016. https://www.historynet.com/portugee-phillips-fort-phil-kearny.

Historical Marker Database. https://www.hmdb.org/m.asp?m=152094; https://www.hmdb.org/m.asp?m=128145.

Hoffman, Phillip A. https://www.environmentandsociety.org/arcadia/american-horses-south-african-war-1899-1902.

International Museum of the Horse. "The Spanish Returns Equus to its Prehistoric Homes—The Perilous Crossing," https://imh.org/exhibits/past/legacy-of-the-horse/spanish-return-equus-its-prehistoric-home.

Kansas State Historical Society. https://www.kshs.org/publicat/khq/1959/1959winter_pony_express.pdf.

Lang, William. "Essay: Oregon Trail." https://www.oregonencyclopedia.org/articles
/oregon_trail/#:~:text=The%20Oregon%20Trail%20developed%20from
,man%20returning%20from%20Fort%20Astor.

Library of Congress. "California as I Saw It: First-Person Narratives of California's
Early Years, 1849 to 1900," https://www.loc.gov/collections/california-first-person
-narratives/articles-and-essays/early-california-history.

Long Riders Guild Academic Foundation. http://www.lrgaf.org/journeys/drives.htm.

Monnett, John H. "The Falsehoods of Fetterman's Fight," October 1, 2010. https://www
.historynet.com/the-falsehoods-of-fettermans-fight.

National Endowment for the Humanities. https://www.neh.gov/humanities/2012/
marchapril/statement/woman-the-west.

National Park Service. https://www.nps.gov/poex/faqs.htm; https://www.nps.gov/
parkhistory/online_books/poex/hrs/hrs3a.htm#:~:text=The%20first
%20division%20ran%20from,from%20Roberts%20Creek%20to%20Sacramento;
https://nationalparktraveling.com/listing/pony-bob-haslam-and-his-famous-pony
-express-rides/#; https://www.nps.gov/waba/learn/historyculture/lt-col-alfred-h
-sully-1821-1879.htm#:~:text=In%20September%20of%201868%2C%20with
,during%20the%20summer%20of%201868.

National Pony Express Association. https://nationalponyexpress.org/historic-pony
-express-trail/stations/#:~:text=The%20Pony%20Express%20Used%20Over
,used%20for%20"The%20Pony."

Oklahoma State University. https://breeds.okstate.edu/horses/quarter-horses.html; http:
//afs.okstate.edu/breeds/horses/cayuseindian/index.html.

Online Etymology Dictionary. "Cavalry," https://www.etymonline.com/word
/breed#etymonline_v_17087; https://www.etymonline.com/word/
cavalry#etymonline_v_8303; https://www.etymonline.com/search?q=horsepower.

Patterson, Michael Robert. "Thomas Tipton Thornburgh – Major, U.S. Army." https://
www.arlingtoncemetery.net/ttthornburgh.htm.

Pierron, G. Joseph. "Lewis Lindsey Dyche." *Kansas Historical Quarterly*. https://www.kshs
.org/kansapedia/lewis-lindsay-dyche/18149.

Pendleton Roundup. https://www.pendletonroundup.com/p/round-up/147.

Plains Indians and Pioneers Museum. https://www.facebook.com/PIPMWoodward/
photos/a.10150836469563717/10159488369033717/?type=3&source=57&locale
=ms_MY&paipv=0&eav=AfYMJx88gGEB9YNMpuxYiaHDajHqC3IXnaRSizS
DdtC6OZzHlFQcsaxuELHvifDY96g&_rdr.

Pro Rodeo. https://prorodeo.com/prorodeo/rodeo/rodeo101/;_https://prorodeo.com/
news/2022/7/31/general-saddle-bronc-rider-logan-hay-registered-world-record
-95-5-point-ride-in-pollockville-win.

Pro Rodeo Hall of Fame. https://www.prorodeohalloffame.com/inductees/livestock/war
-paint/; https://www.prorodeohalloffame.com/inductees/livestock/high-tide.

Rare Historical Photos. https://rarehistoricalphotos.com/vintage-photographs-move
-house-horses.

Schilz, Thomas F. "Battle of Palo Duro Canyon," Texas State Historical Association, August 4, 2020, https://www.tshaonline.org/handbook/entries/palo-duro-canyon -battle-of.

Spokane County. https://www.spokanecounty.org/1070/Saddle-Bronc.

United Service Organizations. https://www.uso.org/stories/2465-9-must-know-facts -about-the-army-s-1st-cavalry-division-for-its-birthday#:~:text =9%20Must-Know%20Facts%20about%20the%20Army%27s%201st%20Cavalry ,to%20Make%20it%20Into%20Manila.%20...%20More%20items.

US Postal Museum. https://postalmuseum.si.edu/exhibition/remember-the-pony/the -oath-of-office.

Western Horseman. https://westernhorseman.com/culture/out-west/the-horses-of-the -pony-express.

Women's Ranch Bronc Championships. https://www.womensranchbronc.com/standings.

NEWSPAPERS

Aspen Weekly Times (Aspen, Colorado)
Billings Gazette (Billings, Montana)
Colorado Daily Chieftain (Pueblo, Colorado)
Daily Camera (Boulder, Colorado)
Daily Enterprise (Livingston, Montana)
Daily Sentinel (Grand Junction, Colorado)
Evansville Journal (Evansville, Indiana)
Great Divide Newspaper (Denver, Colorado)
Helena Weekly Herald (Helena, Montana)
Leadville Weekly Herald (Leadville, Colorado)
New York Times (New York, New York)
Pueblo Chieftain (Colorado)
River Press (Fort Benton, Montana)
Rocky Mountain News (Denver, Colorado)
Sheridan Post (Sheridan, Wyoming)
Sun River Sun (Sun River, Montana)

JOURNAL ARTICLES

Bower, Bruce. "Native Americans Corralled Spanish Horses Decades before Europeans Arrived." *Science News* (March 30, 2023), https://www.sciencenews.org/article/ native-americans-spanish-horses.

Burkey, Elmer R. "The Thornburgh Battle with the Utes on Milk Creek." *Colorado Magazine* 1, 3n3 (May 1936): 90–110, https://www.historycolorado.org/sites/default/ files/media/document/2018/ColoradoMagazine_v13n3_May1936.pdf.

Cantwell, Robert. "The Great 1,000 Mile Race from Chadron to Chicago!" *The Vault: Sports Illustrated*, https://vault.si.com/vault/1962/09/03/the-great-1000mile -race-from-chadron-to-chicago.

Carpenter, John A. "General Howard and the Nez Perce War of 1877." *The Pacific Northwest Quarterly* 49, 4 (1958): 129–45.

Cedarwald, Major A.A. *The Quartermaster Review.* Army Quartermaster Foundation, Inc., November-December 1928. https://www.quartermasterfoundation.org/the-remount-service-past-and-present.

Colorado Encyclopedia. "The Meeker Incident." https://coloradoencyclopedia.org/article/meeker-incident.

Dobie, J. Frank. "Indian Horses and Horsemanship." *Southwest Review* 35, no. 4 (1950): 265–75.

Fleek, Sherman. "Grant in Mexico: One of the Most Unjust (Wars) Ever Waged." (January 31, 2019), https://www.army.mil/article/216806/grant_in_mexico_one_of_the_most_unjust_wars_ever_waged.

Forbes, Jack D. "The Appearance of the Mounted Indian in Northern Mexico and the Southwest, to 1680." *Southwestern Journal of Anthropology* 15, no. 2 (1959): 189–212.

Gandi, Lakshmi. "The Indigenous Roots of Vaqueros—and Cowboys," *History*, August 17, 2023, https://www.history.com/news/mexican-vaquero-american-cowboy.

Gray, John S. "Veterinary Service on Custer's Last Campaign." *Kansas Historical Quarterly* 3, 3 (1977).
https://www.kshs.org/p/veterinary-service-on-custer-s-last-campaign/13275#Note2.

Greenfield, Elizabeth. "A Horse Drive to Montana Territory, 1881." *Montana: The Magazine of Western History* 13, 3 (1963): 18–33.

Hämäläinen, Pekka. "The Rise and Fall of Plains Indian Horse Cultures," https://historycooperative.org/journal/the-rise-and-fall-of-plains-indian-horse-cultures.

Herrick, Dennis. "Xauian and the Tiguex War." *Native Peoples Magazine* (January/February 2014), http://dennisherrick.com/Xau%C3%ADan.

Hughes, Willis B. "The First Dragoons on the Western Frontier 1834-1846." *Arizona and the West* 12, no. 2 (1970): 115–38.

Kilgrove, Kristina. "Indigenous People of the American West Used 'Sacred' Horses a Half-Century Earlier than Previously Thought." *Live Science* (March 30, 2023), https://www.livescience.com/indigenous-people-of-the-american-west-used-sacred-horses-a-half-century-earlier-than-previously-thought.

Lingeman, Jake. "History of the Mustang Logo." *Autoweek* (April 27, 2020), https://www.autoweek.com/car-life/classic-cars/a32266716/history-of-the-mustang-logo.

Lisec, Gianna. "Saddles a Big Part of Pueblo History." *Pueblo Chieftain* (October 5, 2011), https://www.chieftain.com/story/news/2011/10/05/saddles-big-part-pueblo-history/8723934007.

Moody, Marshall D. "The Meeker Massacre." *Colorado Magazine* (April 1952): 96, https://www.historycolorado.org/sites/default/files/media/document/2018/ColoradoMagazine_v30n2_April1953.pdf.

Nixon, Lance. "Bounding Home: Masterpiece of Plains Indian Sculpture returns to South Dakota." (October 8, 2015), https://www.capjournal.com/news/bounding-home-masterpiece-of-plains-indian-sculpture-returns-to-south-dakota/article_85933c9a-6e38-11e5-828e-1f6bf2faad8b.html.

Nye, E.L. "Cavalry Horse." *Montana: The Magazine of Western History* 7, no. 2 (1957): 40–45.

Pohanka, Brian. "Myles Keogh: From the Vatican to the Little Big Horn: A New Biography of the Famous Cavalryman." *Military Images* 8, no. 2 (1986): 15–24.

Rey, Agapito. "The Rodriguez Expedition to New Mexico 1581-1582." *New Mexico Historical Review* 2, 3 (1927): article 3, https://digitalrepository.unm.edu/cgi/viewcontent.cgi?article=1405&context=nmhr.

Settle, Raymond W. "The Pony Express—Heroic Effort, Tragic End." *Utah Historical Quarterly* 27, 2 (1959). https://issuu.com/utah10/docs/uhq_volume27_1959 _number2/s/97343.

Sherow, James E. "Workings of the Geodialectic: High Plains Indians and Their Horses in the Region of the Arkansas River Valley, 1800-1870." *Environmental History Review* 16, no. 2 (1992): 61–84.

Smith, Sharon B. "Vic at the Little Bighorn." *Wild West Magazine: Wild West American Frontier* (June 2022): 32–39.

Stauffer, Alvin P. "Supply of the First American Overseas Expeditionary Force: The Quartermaster's Department and the Mexican War." *Quartermaster Review,* May-June 1950, http://old.quartermasterfoundation.org/quartermaster_department_mexican _war.htm.

Villano, Matt. "Miles City Saddlery is as Smooth as Leather." *Montana Living* (March 10, 2016), https://www.montanaliving.com/blogs/mercantile/112959237-miles -city-saddlery-is-as-smooth-as-leather.

Wooley, David L., and Horse Capture, Joseph D. "Joseph No Two Horns: He Nupe Wanica." *American Indian Art Magazine* (Summer 1993): 34, http://faculty.washington .edu/kbunn/Wooley.pdf.

Worcester, D.E. "The Spread of Spanish Horses in the Southwest." *New Mexico Historical Review* 19, 3 (1944), https://digitalrepository.unm.edu/nmhr/vol19/iss3/3.

ARCHIVES

Ulysses S. Grant, The Personal Memoirs of Ulysses S. Grant, https://www-tc.pbs.org/wgbh/americanexperience/media/filer_public/00/9d/009d03b6 -2f0c-4197-a13d-219044df1182/grant_memoirs.pdf.

Haslam, James H., interview by S.A. Kenner, reported by Josiah Rogerson, December 4, 1884. https://digitalcommons.usu.edu/cgi/viewcontent.cgi?article=2430&context=gradreports.

Young, Brigham, to Isaac C. Haight, September 10, 1857.

Welch Dakota Papers. "Oral History of the Dakotah Tribes 1800s–1945 as Told to Colonel

A.B. Welch First White Man Adopted by the Sioux Nation." https://www .welchdakotapapers.com/2011/11/little-big-horn-general-shermans-command -watching-for-and-searching-for-sitting-bull-january-thru-october-1876/#film -0585.

RADIO/PODCASTS

Idaho Matters. Frankie Barnhill, Senior Producer. June 10, 2021.
https://www.boisestatepublicradio.org/show/idaho-matters/2021-06-10/the-forgotten
-story-of-the-horse-queen-of-idaho.

BLOGS

Homan, Philip A., Idaho State University, Pocatello, Idaho.
https://ruralwomensstudies.wordpress.com/2015/09/16/meeting-miss-kittie-my
-friendship-with-kittie-wilkins-the-horse-queen-of-idaho.